The Mechanics of Ifa Divination System

The Mechanics of Ifa Divination System

Highlighting Some Elements of Technological Knowledge in Ifa and Its Divination System

Ojo Oyebisi

Ajendu LLC

Columbia, Maryland

Published 2019 by Ajendu LLC, Columbia, Maryland.

E-mail: Ajeniju@yahoo.com

Website: Ajendu.blogspot.com

The Mechanics of Ifa Divination System:

Highlighting Some Elements of Technological Knowledge in Ifa and Its Divination System.

ISBN-13: 978-0578517308 (paperback edition)

Acknowledgments

Thanks go first to Debbie Gantt, who advised and encouraged me to write down my ideas about the technological information embedded in the Ifa divination system and publish them in a book. She has endured my journey through stress and excitement. I am grateful to her.

I express my profound gratitude to David Oyegoke (aka Ọlọbẹ Yoyọn), who did not only give me unrestricted access to his online library but also assisted me in writing a computer program for the implementation of the Odu Ifa encryption scheme that I talk about in the last chapter of this book.

Special thanks go to Awo Nathan Lugo, Awo Akomolafe Wande, and Onanuga Ololade for providing me some useful photographs for this project.

I thank my friend, Carla Mofura Hibbert, for sharing with me her insights into the esoteric and cultural information of the Ifa divination system.

Words cannot express my gratitude to my editor, John X. Miller, who was diligent in his efforts in making my words and ideas clearer.

Table of Contents

Introduction

The majority of native Yoruba speakers view the Ifa divination system as a form of dark magic, inconsequential shamanism or ritualistic fetish. Even some scholars of Ifa and its divination system have conveyed the impression that it is simply a primitive oracular instrument of narrative art that should be appreciated only for its poetic sublimity. The Ifa divination system has been greatly misconceived as a mere esoteric system, devoid of any form of technological information.

The purpose of this work, therefore, is to describe what the Ifa divination system truly is and to illustrate its pertinence to modern information technology.

The road to understanding what the Ifa divination system truly is requires one to view it not only as cultural-level information but also as technological-level information. From my observation, traditional practitioners, who are the custodians of the esoteric knowledge of Ifa and its divination system, do not understand the sequential order of the evolution of knowledge. As a result, they do not know how to extract technological-level information from their cultural knowledge of Ifa and its divination system. The African scholars; on the other hand, who understand the sequential order of the evolution of knowledge do not have enough knowledge of the cultural information in Ifa and its divination system to even attempt to enhance technological development with this information.

It is my goal, in this didactic book, to expand on the operation and structure of the Ifa divination system and highlight some of the elements of technological knowledge that are embedded in both.

HOW TO READ THIS BOOK

I wrote *The Mechanics of Ifa Divination System* to be both a lively introduction to some of the technological-level information in Ifa divination system and a concise reference for those who are interested in enhancing technological development within the context of the cultural knowledge of Ifa and its divination system. This book is not intended to be a religious text, nor is it intended to rehash some of the cultural information in Ifa and its divination system. In other words, this book cannot teach readers how to become a Babalawo, an Ifa priest or diviner. One cannot read a book or a collection of books and become a Babalawo. To become a Babalawo, one has to be initiated into the Ifa priesthood and study Ifa and its divination system for many years. Although I have not disregarded the cultural information in Ifa and its divination system, I have attempted, in this book, to show some of the technological-level information in both systems.

This work is divided into ten chapters with two appendixes.

Chapter One points out the sequential order in the evolution or advancement of knowledge. It describes the five stages in the evolution of knowledge and how each stage influences the next. The ultimate aim of this chapter is to show that while scientific or technological knowledge is universal, its development often starts from a local point in one's environment.

Chapter Two focuses generally on what Ifa is. Structurally, Ifa is very complex but this chapter attempts to simplify and explain the scope and structure of Ifa. It gives us the opportunity to settle the controversy surrounding the meaning of Ifa: whether Ifa and Ifa divination system can be used interchangeably to refer to the Yoruba traditional religion.

Chapter Three deals generally with the scope of the Ifa divination system. It explains what the Ifa divination system is. It avails us the opportunity to settle the controversy surrounding the origin of the Ifa divination system: whether it was invented in Africa by the Yoruba people or it was invented in a foreign land by foreigners, who exported the knowledge into Yorubaland. It also examines the structure and descriptive mechanics of the Ifa divination system.

Chapter Four focuses on the order of seniority in the Odu Ifa corpus. It looks at the 16 books and the 256 chapters in the Odu Ifa literary corpus and ranks each chapter according to its descending order of seniority in the Odu Ifa corpus.

Chapter Five examines, in detail, the general process and practice of Ifa divination. It looks at some of the common divinatory techniques that are used by the Babalawo during the divination process and the key differences between these techniques. It also describes some of the well-known instruments of Ifa divination and how they are adapted for divination process.

Chapter Six describes the two traditional number systems, binary and hexadecimal numbers, that are found in the Ifa divination system. It also looks at how these number systems aid the operation of the Ifa divination system.

Chapter Seven deals with a comparative study on the Ifa divination system and digital computer systems. It introduces us to some of the similarities between the operational structure of the Ikin, a divinatory instrument, and a digital computer system. It also shows how each of the 256 Odu Ifa signatures maps to each of the 256 ASCII characters on our computer keyboard.

Chapter Eight focuses on a comparative study on the Ifa divination system and quantum computer systems. It introduces us to some of the similarities between the operational structure of the Ọpẹlẹ quantum chain and quantum computer systems. It also touches on some elements of quantum mechanics in the Ifa divination system; particularly, in the operation and structure of the Ọpẹlẹ quantum chain.

Chapter Nine highlights the key role the Ifa divination system plays in the probabilistic modeling of the human decision-making process. It delves briefly into choice theory and the common differences between choice and decision-making process. It describes, in detail, the adaptation of the Ifa divination system for aiding the decision-making process.

Chapter Ten focuses on the practical application of the Ifa divination system in cryptography. It shows how the Ifa divination system is an excellent pseudo-random number generator. It also describes the development and implementation of the Ọpẹlẹ quchain algorithm for use in encrypting and decrypting data.

Epilogue deals with a general comment as to why Ifa and its divination system must be embraced, properly studied and promoted.

Appendix A shows the implementation of the Ọpẹlẹ quchain algorithm with a python programming language.

Appendix B shows the Odubetical chart, which is a chart of the 256 chapters of Odu Ifa mapped to the 256 ASCII characters on our computer keyboard.

Chapter One

The sequential order of the evolution of scientific and technological knowledge

In one of my posts on social media, I implored my friends to study Ifa and the Ifa divination system and transform the cultural information embedded in both to technological-level information. Unfortunately, most of my friends on social media, who are predominantly Africans, dismissed the cultural information embedded in Ifa and its divination system for having no technological value. Then it dawned on me that most of my friends, perhaps due to colonialization, had lost touch with their cultural information (i.e. myths, dictums, visual arts, spirituality, religion, etc.). Seemingly, they could no longer recognize the link between their cultural information and technological information, nor could they understand how scientific and technological knowledge evolve sequentially as cultural information from one's environment to technological information for the benefit of all mankind.

According to my friends on social media, "science and technology are universal; thus, their development cannot be tied to any regionalized cultural information." I do agree that universalism is rooted deeply in the impersonal nature of science—that is, science is indeed universal with respect to the fact that objectively-proven scientific principles are the same everywhere irrespective of country, region, society or culture. However, if observation is a key factor that drives scientific inquiry and necessity is a key factor that drives technological innovation, then the development of scientific and technological knowledge usually starts from a local perspective. After all, it is in one's immediate environment that one tends to make observations and seek solutions to basic life problems. In other words, although science and technology have universal potentials, their initial development is often localized. For example, legend has it that Newton's observation of a falling apple in his garden inspired the understanding of gravitational force and the subsequent development of the scientific theory of universal gravitation. Similarly, Darwin's sojourn in Galapagos Island certainly inspired his understanding of human evolution and the subsequent development of the scientific theory of natural selection. Furthermore, it is believed by many scholars that the natural cyclical flooding pattern of the Nile River in ancient Egypt was what led the Egyptians to the development of a water management system known as basin irrigation.

Consequently, I maintain that the close proximity between human knowledge and human experience can be seen as the close proximity between an individual and their environment. I propose therefore to proceed, in this chapter, according to the following plan. First, I define what knowledge is, describe the two basic requirements of knowledge and explain briefly the two competing traditions concerning the ultimate source of knowledge. Second, I shall define the sequential order in the evolution of scientific and technological knowledge and describe the stages in the sequential order. Lastly, I shall attempt to illustrate, in a practical perspective, the evolution of scientific and technological knowledge. The ultimate aim is to show that, while scientific or technological knowledge is universal, its development often starts from a local point in our environment. Before I proceed, I must mention very quickly that, for simplicity, the term scientific knowledge will be used interchangeably with technological knowledge.

What is knowledge?

There are different definitions of knowledge. To some people, knowledge is a way of getting at the truth. To many others, knowledge is the fact or condition of being aware of something. However, I have drawn my definition of knowledge from the field of philosophy. So, to me, knowledge may be defined simply as justified true belief. Based on this simple definition, one can conclude that there are three basic requirements of knowledge: belief, truth, and justification.

Belief – A reasonable claim to knowledge must carry an element of belief—that is, one must believe something in order to have some knowledge of it.

Truth – To attribute knowledge to someone is to credit that person with having got things right, and that means what we regard that person as knowing had better not be false, but true. In other words, one must not only believe in something, but the belief must also correspond with reality and must be true.

Justification – It is not enough to just believe; one's belief must be premised on a justifiable reason.

Suppose, for example, I used to live in New York City. A friend of mine, who is currently vacationing in New York City, just called me, asking for a recommendation about a good Italian restaurant in and around Times Square. Having once lived in New York City and worked in and around Times Square, I could honestly say that I know of a good Italian restaurant around Times Square. However, the only way I can justify my belief and substantiate my knowledge of a good Italian restaurant in and around Times Square is to do the following: give my friend the name of the restaurant, the address of the restaurant and perhaps the phone number of the restaurant. This would mean that my friend can call this restaurant, make a reservation, travel to this restaurant, and thereby achieve their goal of dining in a good Italian restaurant in New York City. Only then can I say for certain that I have knowledge of a good Italian restaurant in and around Times Square in New York City. Consequently, true belief does not necessarily correspond to knowledge. For true belief to become genuine knowledge, it must be justified.

Now that we have some understanding of what knowledge is, let us look at the possible sources of our knowledge. There are two competing traditions concerning the source of our knowledge: empiricism and rationalism.

Empiricism

Empiricism refers to those aspects of our knowledge that are derived from our senses or our experiences and not from our reasoning, reflection or intuition. Empiricism fits well with the scientific worldview that places an emphasis on experimentation and observation, especially sensory perception, in the formation of ideas. Consequently, it can be said that scientific knowledge is empirical in nature—that is, our knowledge of science is derived from our experiences or observations.

Rationalism

Rationalism refers to those aspects of our knowledge of reality that are derived from reasoning, reflection or intuition. This school of thought places an emphasis on the operation of the mind in the acquisition of knowledge of reality but down plays the role of senses and experiences in the process of knowledge acquisition.

So, while the two aforementioned opposing worldviews are convincing, it is undeniable that scientific or technological knowledge is a valuable factor, necessarily and inextricably linked to human observation and experience.

The stages in the development of technological knowledge.

A study of the growth of knowledge systems, from the historical perspective, reveals a general trend from mysticism or spirituality to philosophical and subsequently to scientific and technological approaches. The question now is, how does technological knowledge develop from its local point of conception to high-value technological information for the benefit of everybody? In other words, what are the stages in the developmental process of technological knowledge? Before I answer this question, let me briefly expand on what I mean by the sequential order of the evolution of technological knowledge.

The sequential order of the evolution of technological knowledge is the ascending path that the evolution of technological knowledge follows. Generally, it starts as medium-value cultural information, such as myths, dictums, proverbs, visual arts, spirituality, religion, etc., which is restricted to a specific region or subculture and is valuable only to a specific local group of people. And it evolves into high-value technological information, such as science and technology, which is open to all cultures and valuable to all groups of people equally. There are five different stages in the sequential order of the evolution of technological knowledge, and they are as follows in ascending order:

1. The environment
2. Psychology
3. Mythology
4. Philosophy
5. Science and technology

In the sequential order of the evolution of knowledge, the environment is anterior to everything else—that is, it is from our environment that we first observe and learn about the world. And in the quest to understand the world around us better, we tend to raise questions about some of the things we observe—that is, we raise questions about the weather, the sky, the celestial bodies, plants, animals and other things we see in nature.

The relational correspondence between the human environment and the ecology of it represents the basic precondition of human psychology: the environment is everything that affects the individual except his genes. There are many potential environmental influences that help to shape human personality. These include the place we live, the ecology of our environment and our experiences. It has been hypothesized that the climatic condition of one's environment influences one's psychology.

For instance, the people in a cold region usually have to plan ahead to stay warm in the winter months. The cold climate presumably makes people rather practical, competitive and conservative. Conversely, people in a tropical region, where the weather is consistently warm throughout the year, need not plan ahead as much as those who live in a cold region. Consequently, people in a warm climate might be more likely to be cooperative and less likely to be practical, competitive and conservative than those in a cold climate. Now if our environment and the ecology of our environment largely shape our psychology, then our psychology has to shape our mythology. Our mythology, in turn, shapes our philosophy. And lastly, our philosophy shapes our science and technology.

From the foregoing description of the sequential order of the evolution of technological knowledge, it is very clear that the developmental stages in the evolution of technological knowledge are interdependent. And to illustrate this obvious interdependence, in a practical perspective, I shall dig into the Yoruba oral literature, i.e., Yoruba cultural information.

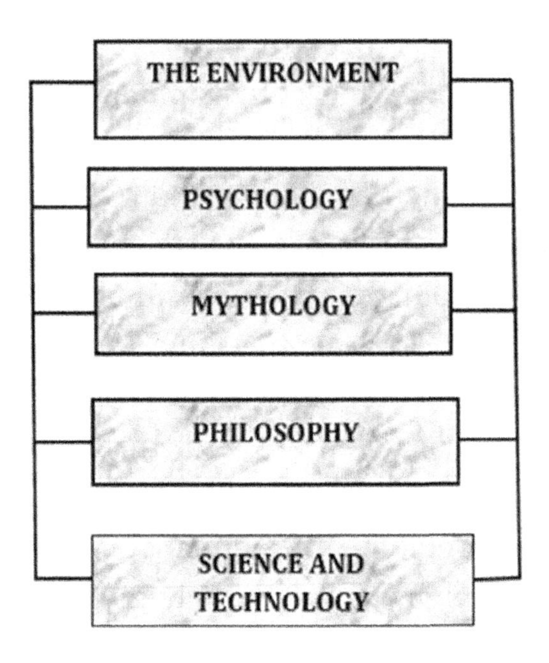

Figure 1. The interdependence of the developmental stages of scientific/technological knowledge

Yoruba dicta and proverbs are commonly used as pedagogical tools for the transmission of knowledge. Tunde Adegbola, a language technologist and the Director of African Languages Technology Initiative (Alt-i), seems to corroborate this when he writes:

> The Yoruba have depended heavily on oral texts for the documentation and organization of knowledge. ... One of the basic tasks in the practice of science is

> the documentation of observations. Yoruba verbal arts are known to fulfill didactic, aesthetic and ritual roles. Spiritual forces are usually attributed to the efficacy of potent speech forms such as ọfọ̀, àyájọ́, èpè and ìwúre. However, many Yoruba proverbs and other literary devices fulfill the basic task of documenting observations as scientific facts. (Falola and Oyebade, 2011, pp. 28 & 31).

For example, the Yoruba dictum; tibi tire la da ile aye, which may be equated to the English saying "reality is a dynamic union of complementary opposites" is a simple expression of the concept of binary complementarity or complementary dualism. In other words, the Yoruba believe that all opposites—odd and even, good and evil, fortune and misfortune, are complementary. So, it is common knowledge among the Yoruba that reality is governed by two opposing forces: ire (fortune or good) and ibi (misfortune or evil). This knowledge is further evident in one of the Yoruba myths, which deals with two farmers, who are good friends, and a prominent Yoruba Oriṣa (deity) called Eṣu.

The myth goes as follows:

> two friends swear undying fidelity to one another but neglect to acknowledge Eshu in their vow. So one day Eshu appears, and takes a stroll between their two plots of land, wearing a cap that is black

> one side and red (or white) on the other. As he saunters along the dividing line, he chats with both men. Afterwards, the two farmers discuss the man with the cap, and fall to violet quarreling about the color of his hat, calling each other blind and crazy. The neighbors gather around, and then Eshu arrives to stop the fight. The friends explain their disagreement, and Eshu shows them the two-sided hat, and chastises them for not putting him first in their doings. (Davis, 2010, pp. 140-141).

Implicit in the above myth are the following:

1. The two-sided cap (red and black) is a metaphor for the binary nature of human reality (i.e. tibi tire).
2. Opposites are part of a unified whole.
3. The dividing line between the two plots of land symbolizes Oritamẹta (the crossroad), where life decisions are made—every decision is a crossroad.
4. Eṣu sometimes creates chaos to show the false fabrications of oppositional ordering and reveal the underlying harmony.
5. True belief may originate from sense-perception, but true knowledge rests on having adequate information.

As the above myth embodies the nature and dialectic of the jointly competing relationship of opposites, it explains the inherent binary nature of human choice and the crucial need for the refinement of human knowledge and choice through information mining.

It is fitting, therefore, that the metaphysical concept of tibi tire would be the bedrock of the conceptual binary framework of the Yoruba worldview and the foundation of the technological knowledge of the Ifa divination system. In her book, "Socrates and Ọrunmila," Oluwole (2017) states:

> the Yoruba nation made one of the greatest contributions to world intellectual heritage. They are one of the first people on earth to formulate, develop and adopt Binary Complementarity as a cogent intellectual structure within which science, philosophy, and the social sciences, severally and jointly, find an existence that is both rational and scientific. (p. 176).

In agreeing with Oluwole's submission, the concept of tibi tire is not only an ontological dictum, it has broad applicability in quantum science. In fact, Niels Bohr, the famous Danish physicist, stated in one of his collected works in quantum physics that binary complementarity was a principle of physics and the bedrock of quantum mechanics.

In conclusion, we must bear in mind that the development of technological knowledge is not coincidental or arbitrary. It follows a strict sequential order with interconnected developmental stages. In this sequential order, our psychology is connected to the ecology of our environment. Our mythology is connected to our psychology. Our philosophy is connected to our mythology. And our technology is connected to our philosophy. Accordingly, if our psychology is underdeveloped, then our mythology would be underdeveloped. If our mythology is underdeveloped, then our philosophy would be underdeveloped. And lastly, if our philosophy is underdeveloped, then our science and technology would certainly be underdeveloped. I cannot stress it enough: we must research and study every subject in our cultural knowledge base to enhance our technological development.

Chapter Two

What is Ifa?

In Yorubaland and in nearly all the Yoruba's diasporic communities among them, Brazil, Trinidad and Tobago, Cuba, and Puerto Rico, Ifa has been reduced to cultural-level information. Today, the majority of native Yoruba speakers and most people around the world regard Ifa as the Yoruba traditional religion. It is a curious phenomenon that even scholars of Ifa are divided on the true meaning of Ifa. Many scholars of Ifa suggest that Ifa is nothing more than a religious and mythic discourse. Some argue that Ifa is a form of philosophy while others think Ifa is simply a divination system. So is Ifa a form of religion, philosophy or divination system?

Ifa is a very complex system with many different aspects or essences. It is very important that we first and foremost understand the different aspects of Ifa before we can begin to define and understand what Ifa truly is. In his lecture on what is Ifa, Odeyemi (n.d.) suggests the following:

> A thorough study of the ramifications of Ifa shows that it comprises eight basic essences listed as follows:
>
> I. **The Spiritual Essence**: this relates to the place of man (as a spirit) in the cosmos, the powers of matter and all aspects of ontological evolution and development.
>
> II. **The Religious Essence**: this relates to faith, catechism and Ifagelism (Preaching).
>
> III. **The Divine Essence**: this relates to the methods of divination and accessing of esoteric information; the mechanics of divination and the systematics of divine message collection, processing and interpretation.
>
> IV. **The Worship and Sacrificial Essence**: this relates to the basis and meaning of worship and sacrifice.
>
> V. **The Medicinal Essence**: this deals with both magical and materialist medicine.
>
> VI. **The Historical Essence**: this deals with the history of all creation, including the creation of materialist, non-materialist and spirit worlds.

> VII. **The Scientific Essence**: this deals with the power of observation, axiomatic, astronomy, cosmology, cognitive and pre-cognitive experience, astral science, physical and biological sciences, logic, philosophy, mathematics, statistics and computer science.
>
> VIII. **The Cultural Essence**: this relates to rites, rituals, politics, socio-economics, language, dress and normative value systems.
>
> As it is obvious, ... Religion, Worship and Sacrifice are but a few aspects of what constitute the Divine Message known as Ifa. (p. 6).

Considering the eight essences of Ifa, suggested above, it is obvious that peoples' views about Ifa are shaped by the aspect or essence of Ifa they are familiar with—that is, since people are not familiar with all aspects of Ifa, they tend to define Ifa narrowly from their vantage points. I am not here to contest any of the narrow definitions that people may have about Ifa. I think it is proper, however, to give Ifa its broadest reasonable definition, one which encompasses all its different aspects. Consequently, I have chosen to define Ifa as the literary corpus of Yoruba mythology, history, spirituality, moral ethics, cosmology, metaphysics, philosophy and science/technology. In other words, Ifa is the dynamic knowledge base of Yoruba experience, which can be relied upon to reconstruct the worldview of the Yoruba.

The scope and structure of Ifa

According to Bascom (1969):

> Ifa is a system of divination based on 16 basic and 256 derivative figures (Odu) obtained either by the manipulation of sixteen sacred palm nuts (ikin), or by the toss of the divination chain (Ọpẹlẹ) of eight half seed shells. (p. 3).

A number of scholars, like Bascom, find it difficult to separate Ifa from its divination system. In fact, they often use the two terms interchangeably. It is true that Ifa does have divination as a significant component, but Ifa is by no means limited to its divination system. While Ifa is the dynamic knowledge base of Yoruba experience, the Ifa divination system is a practical tool adapted for organizing, processing and retrieving the vast information that is reposited in the Ifa literary corpus. Ifa and its divination system are collectively used as a decision-making tool, although in different forms in West Africa, the Americas and the Canary Islands. They are central to the traditions of Santeria, Vodou and Candomble.

For simplicity, Ifa literary corpus can be organized into 16 books with 256 different chapters—there are 16 principal or major chapters (Oju Odu) and 240 minor chapters (Ọmọ Odu) of Odu Ifa. The

256 chapters, in the Ifa literary corpus, are collectively called the Odu Ifa or simply Odu. In other words, the whole of the Ifa literary corpus is based on the Odu Ifa. The following is a list of all the 16 books in the entire Ifa literary corpus and the corresponding number of chapters in each book:

1. Book one is the book of Ogbe; it has 31 chapters.
2. Book two is the book of Ọyẹku; it has 29 chapters.
3. Book three is the book of Iwori; it has 27 chapters.
4. Book four is the book of Odi; it has 25 chapters.
5. Book five is the book of Irosun; it has 23 chapters.
6. Book six is the book of Ọwọnrin; it has 21 chapters.
7. Book seven is the book of Ọbara; it has 19 chapters.
8. Book eight is the book of Ọkanran; it has 17 chapters.
9. Book nine is the book of Ogunda; it has 15 chapters.
10. Book ten is the book of Ọsa; it has 13 chapters.

11. Book eleven is the book of Ika; it has 11 chapters.
12. Book twelve is the book of Oturupọn; it has 9 chapters.
13. Book thirteen is the book of Otura; it has 7 chapters.
14. Book fourteen is the book of Irẹtẹ; it has 5 chapters.
15. Book fifteen is the book of Ọsẹ; it has 3 chapters.
16. Book sixteen is the book of Ofun; it has 1 chapter.

Each one of the 16 books and 256 chapters of Odu Ifa has its own binary-based signature. Table 1 and table 2 show the hierarchical chart of the 16 books in the Ifa literary corpus with their binary signatures and their corresponding binary numbers.

I I I I Book 1. Ogbe	II II II II Book 2. Oyẹku	II I I II Book 3. Iwori	I II II I Book 4. Odi
I I II II Book 5. Irosun	II II I I Book 6. Ọwọnrin	I II II II Book 7. Ọbara	II II II I Book 8. Ọkanran
I I I II Book 9. Ogunda	II I I I Book 10. Ọsa	II I II II Book 11. Ika	II II I II Book 12. Oturupọn
I II I I Book 13. Otura	I I II I Book 14. Iretẹ	I II I II Book 15. Osẹ	II I II I Book 16. Ofun

Table 1. The 16 books in the Ifa corpus and their symbolic signatures.

0 0 0 0 Book 1. Ogbe	1 1 1 1 Book 2. Oyẹku	1 0 0 1 Book 3. Iwori	0 1 1 0 Book 4. Odi
0 0 1 1 Book 5. Irosun	1 1 0 0 Book 6. Ọwọnrin	0 1 1 1 Book 7. Ọbara	1 1 1 0 Book 8. Ọkanran
0 0 0 1 Book 9. Ogunda	1 0 0 0 Book 10. Ọsa	1 0 1 1 Book 11. Ika	1 1 0 1 Book 12. Oturupọn
0 1 0 0 Book 13. Otura	0 0 1 0 Book 14. Iretẹ	0 1 0 1 Book 15. Osẹ	1 0 1 0 Book 16. Ofun

Table 2. The 16 books in the Ifa corpus and their equivalent binary signatures.

Each chapter of Odu Ifa is composed of a vast number of Ifa verses (ẹsẹ Ifa)—some scholars put the number of verses in each chapter of Odu Ifa at around 1,680; some say the number is unknown. According to Abimbola (1997):

> The whole of the literary corpus known as ẹsẹ Ifa is based on the Odu. ... each Odu contains an unspecified number of ẹsẹ. ... the ẹsẹ form the main bulk of chants in the Ifa literary corpus. (p. 31).

The Odu Ifa verses are a compendium of information on Yoruba mythology, spirituality, moral ethics, cosmology, epistemology, metaphysics, philosophy and medicine. This information pervades the Yoruba worldview throughout history. Abimbola captures this point as follows:

> Ẹsẹ Ifa deals with all subjects. It deals with history, geography, religion, music and philosophy. Ẹsẹ Ifa may be a simple story about a man going on a journey and asking for advice on how to make the journey successful. It may be a highly philosophical story showing the merits and demerits of monogamy. It may deal with the foundation of a particular town. There is certainly no limit to the subject matter which ẹsẹ Ifa may deal with. (p. 32).

In style and structure, the Odu Ifa verses are rendered in poetic form. These poems vary in length, some have a few lines while others have hundreds of lines. It can, therefore, be said that there is a sublime literary tradition identifiable in the Ifa literary corpus. Consequently, to illustrate the structure and poetic sublimity of Ifa verses, I have chosen a poem from Ogbe Ofun, one of the minor chapters of Odu Ifa. This poem is directed toward good fortune of wealth, wives, and children and reads as follows:

Agbe rele
Agbe rode
Abe gegeege roja Ejigbomekun
A dia fun Owo lelewa
Ti n torun bow aye
Won ni gbogbo ohun taaa fii se fuja ni ko rubo si
Ko le baa ni won lopolopo
Beeyan o ba lowo lowo
Ko daa
Bi o ba laya
Ko wulo
Beeyan o bimo
Ko kaye ja
Bi o rile gbe
O buru jai
Won ni ebo ni ko ru
Ngba to Owo lelewa rubo
Aye ye e
O lowo lowo
O laya
O bimo

O kole
Ni wa n jo n ni n yo
Ni n yin awon Babalawo
Awon Babalawo n yin Ifa
O ni bee lawon Babalawo toun wi
Agbe rele
Agbe rode
Agbe gegeege roja Ejigbomekun
A dia fun Owo lelewa
Ti n torun bo waye
Ase owo lewa oun aya
Eeya e e se fuja lai lowo
Owo lewa oun aya
Ile lewaoun omo
Eeyan e e se fuja lai nile
Ile lewa oun omo

The English translation of the above poem reads:

It was carried home
It was carried out
It was carried aloft to the market of Ejigbomekun
Cast divination for Owo Lelewa
That was coming to the earth from heaven
He was asked to perform sacrifice
He was told to offer sacrifice for all things necessary for use as showoff in life
Such that he could have them all in abundance
If one has no money
It is not good
If one has no wife
It is awkward
If one has no child

He has only passed through life as a sightseer
If he cannot find a house to live in
It is disturbing
He was asked to perform sacrifice
Life pleased him
He had so much money
He had wives
He had children
He also built many houses
He then started to dance and rejoice
He was praising his Babalawos
His Babalawos were praising Ifa
He said it was exactly as his Babalawos predicted
It was carried home
It was carried out
It was carried aloft to the market of Ejigbomekun
Cast divination for Owo lelewa
That was coming to the earth from heaven
Therefore money is the beauty in conjunction with the wife
No one sets for a showoff without having money
Wealth is the beauty in conjunction with the wife
Therefore the house is the beauty in conjunction with the children
No one sets for a showoff without having a house
The house is the beauty in conjunction with the children
(Salami, 2002, pp. 50-51).

Chapter Three

Ifa divination system

The Ifa divination system is a robust binary-based system that is employed by the Yoruba people of West Africa and other Ifa adherents around the world to organize, store, process and retrieve information from the Ifa knowledge base. As I previously mentioned in chapter two, the information in the Ifa literary corpus can be organized into 16 books with 256 chapters, which are collectively called Odu or Odu Ifa. The 256 chapters in the Odu Ifa literary corpus comprise 16 major chapters and 240 minor chapters; each chapter, as each book, has its unique signature or address.

In terms of my knowledge of information management system, the Ifa divination system can be described as a hierarchical database that comprises 256 data tables. Each data table or Odu Ifa has a unique signature and name, and within each of the 256 Odu Ifa data tables, there are around 1,680 sacred Ifa verses. Thus, the body of Ifa literary corpus consists of 430,080 messages, comprising information about Yoruba myths, spirituality, moral ethics, cosmology, metaphysics, philosophy and science/technology.

Traditionally, the Babalawo commits the verses, in the Odu Ifa literary corpus, to memory. During the divinatory process, the Babalawo generates random signatures using the divinatory instruments such as the Ikin (the 16 sacred palm nuts) or the Ọpẹlẹ quantum chain—there are 256 possible signatures that can be generated. The Babalawo queries the Odu Ifa data tables in memory with the generated signatures and recites, from memory, the verses in the Odu Ifa data tables that correspond to the generated signatures. According to Abimbola (1997):

> By far the most part of the work of the student Ifa divination priests is learning by heart of a number of ẹsẹ from each of the two hundred and fifty-six Odu. Particular attention is paid to the principal sixteen Odu which are also the first sixteen Odu in the

> corpus. There seems to be no fixed number of ẹsẹ which each trainee must learn before he qualifies for initiation, but most of my informants confirm that in ancient times, nobody would be respected as a good Ifa priest unless he has learnt by heart at least sixteen ẹsẹ in each of the two hundred and fifty-six Odu. (pp. 19-20).

Today, the body of Odu Ifa literary corpus can be stored in an electronic storage medium and accessed when needed during the divination process.

The origin of Ifa divination system

The proponents of the foreign conception model argue that the Ifa divination system was conceived outside of Africa and was later imported into Yorubaland. Some argue that the Ifa divination system originated as a derivative of the Chinese I Ching system, from the Far East. Some even argue that it is a derivative of ilm al-raml, the Arabic sand cutting divination system. However, the proponents of the local conception model maintain that the Ifa divination system was conceived in Yorubaland, and it was from Yorubaland that the knowledge spread to the rest of Africa and the world.

According to one of the Yoruba oral traditions, the Ifa divination system was introduced to the Yoruba people of Ọyọ at a late period by Alaafin (King) Onigbogi of the Old Ọyọ Kingdom (circa 1500s), who was said to have been dethroned for having introduced Ifa to his people. Another Yoruba oral tradition states that the Ifa divination system was introduced into the Yoruba-land by a blind man called Ṣetilu, a native of Nupe Land, who initiated many of his followers in the mysteries of the Ifa divination system. According to a popular Yoruba myth, Olodumare (the Yoruba Godhead) is said to have given the power of divination to Ọrunmila (the Ọrisa of wisdom and divination). Ọrunmila subsequently used this power to invent the Ifa divination system, thousands of years ago, for the benefit of all man-kind.

It is true that in complexity, structure and poetic sublimity, the Ifa divination system is very similar to Chinese I Ching. In fact, outside of Africa, Chinese I Ching is the most similar divination system to the Ifa divination system. However, the Ifa divination system is a binary-based tetragram system ($2^4 = 16$) while the Chinese I Ching is a binary-based trigram system ($2^3 = 8$). So, it is safe to logically conclude that the Chinese I Ching is a subset of the Ifa system, for its trigram system is subsumed under the tetragram system of the Ifa divination system.

Structurally, the Ifa divination system is also similar to Arabic ilm al-raml; yet, markedly different. The Ifa divination system and Arabic ilm al-raml use similar markings or symbols, and their signatures are both read from right to left. However, their logical operations are rather different. For example, in the Ifa divination system, a double mark (**II**) represents binary 1 or odd while a single mark (**I**) represents binary 0 or even; this is the opposite of Arabic ilm al-raml. Another obvious difference is that every Odu, in the Ifa divination system, is accompanied with elaborate myths and poetic verses upon which the interpretation of the Odu or Odu Ifa depends. Arabic ilm al-raml, by contrast, is associated with astrology; it has no myths or poetic verses. Clearly, the Ifa divination system and Arabic ilm al-raml are markedly different. It is exasperating that in spite of the notable differences between the Ifa divination system and Arabic ilm al-raml, the proponents of the foreign conception model continue to argue the Ifa divination system is a derivative of Arabic ilm al-raml. Although the two systems might have borrowed from each other in the distant past, there is no evidence the Ifa divination system originated from ilm al-raml.

While there is no consensus on the historical origin of the Ifa divination system, I suggest since the concept of binary is central to the operation and structure of the Ifa divination system, it is not unlikely that the Ifa divination system was conceived in Yorubaland based on the Yoruba's binary worldview of tibi tire. We find in Odu Eji-Ogbe, the king of all the Odu in the Ifa literary corpus, a verse that references doubling in the process of Ifa divination:

> Eji eji ni mo gbe,
> N o gbe enikan mo
> A dia fun Tayewo,
> A bu fun keyinde
>
> I bless in twos,
> I do not bless only one
> Divined for Tayewo,
> He that shares with his Keyinde. (Ajayi, n.d., pp. 57-58).

It is well known that Africans use a number system in which they count by multiples of two—that is, doubling is fundamental to many of the counting systems in Africa, even today. In agreement with my assertion, Eglash (1999) states:

> It is true that many cases of African arithmetic are based on multiples of two ... The presence of doubling as a cultural theme occurs in many African societies, and in many social domains, connecting the sacredness of twins, spirit doubles, and double vision with material objects ... (p. 89).

Consequently, I maintain that the dualistic or binary aspect of the ancient African worldview, as evidenced in the Yoruba philosophical dictum of tibi tire, might have led to the conception and development of the Ifa divination system.

Descriptive mechanics of the Ifa divination system

1. A conceptual focus on "two-truths" or complementarity (tibi tire).
2. Mathematical forecast of ibi and ire using "odd" and "even" counts or the exponential power of 2.
3. A basic dichotomy of ibi and ire framed as two mutually exclusive propositions.
4. The arrangement and manipulation of symbolic or binary signatures (**I or 0** and **II or 1**), in a 4x2 matrix structure, to forecast the outcome of each proposition.
5. The use of Ikin or the 4x2 Ọpẹlẹ quantum chain as a divinatory instrument.
6. Simple procedures of random casting, iteration and elimination.
7. A propensity for the number 2 and its repeated duplication (2, 4, 8...... 2^n).
8. A data repository of all the 256 mathematically possible binary combinations (Odu Ifa) with their accompanying poetic verses.

9. Hierarchical classification of all the 256 Odu Ifa into two groups: 16 major Odu Ifa and 240 minor Odu Ifa.
10. Reliance on the above hierarchy for divinatory computation.
11. Each Odu Ifa, regardless of class and hierarchy, is equiprobable and is randomly generated by chance.
12. Extensive use of idioms, axioms, poems and myths.

Understanding the structure of the Ifa divination system and the legs of Odu Ifa

The Ifa divination system is a system of lines, symbols, tetragrams and octagrams. Lines form the basic unit of the Ifa divination system in that it is from drawing vertical lines that we create the two symbols or marks of Ifa: "I" and "II,' where the symbol "I" corresponds to binary number 0 and the symbol "II" corresponds to binary number 1. By combining the two symbols, we can create the unique signature of every book and every chapter in the Ifa literary corpus.

The Ifa divination system is structured in a binary format in its organization and application of knowledge. Structurally, the Ifa divination system can be represented as a 4x2 entangled-bit matrix, comprising four rows and two columns, where the two columns are the two legs of Odu Ifa.

A	B
0/1	0/1
0/1	0/1
0/1	0/1
0/1	0/1

Left leg = Ai = (i=1....16)
Right leg = Bi = (i=1....16)

Each leg can have $2^4 = 16$ possible outcomes. So, when the left and the right legs are iteratively combined, there are $2^4 \times 2^4 = 2^8 = 256$ possible outcomes.

The Ifa divination system has 256 leading signatures of which 16 are bilaterally symmetric, having identical right and left legs, and the remaining 240 signatures are bilaterally asymmetric, having non-identical right and left legs. Each of the signatures addresses a specific chapter in the Ifa literary corpus. The symmetric signatures address the major chapters of Odu Ifa, which are also called the Eji or Meji Odu: Eji-Ogbe or Ogbe-Meji, Ọyẹku-Meji, Iwori-Meji, Odi-Meji, Irosun-Meji, Ọwọnrin-Meji, Ọbara-Meji, Ọkanran-Meji, Ogunda-Meji, Ọsa-Meji, Ika-Meji, Oturupọn-Meji, Otura-

Meji, Irẹtẹ-Meji, Ọsẹ-Meji and Ofun-Meji (see tables 3 and 4). For instance, Eji-Ogbe is one of the major chapters of Odu Ifa and its symmetric signature can be represented as:

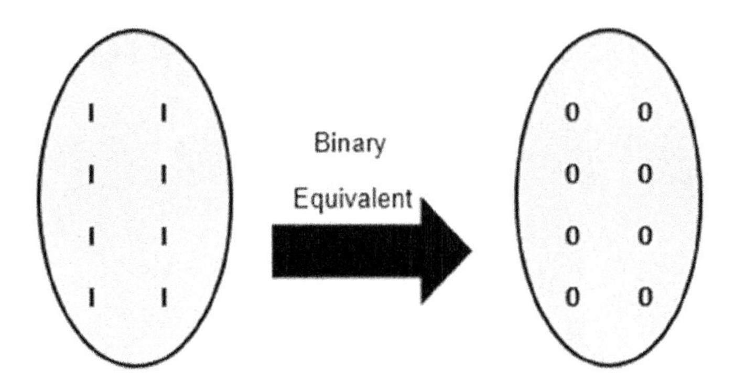

Figure 2. A schematic of Odu Eji-Ogbe's symmetric signature and its binary equivalent

Conversely, the asymmetric signatures address the minor chapters of Odu Ifa. For instance, Ogbe-Ọbara is one of the minor chapters of Odu Ifa, and its asymmetric signature can be represented as:

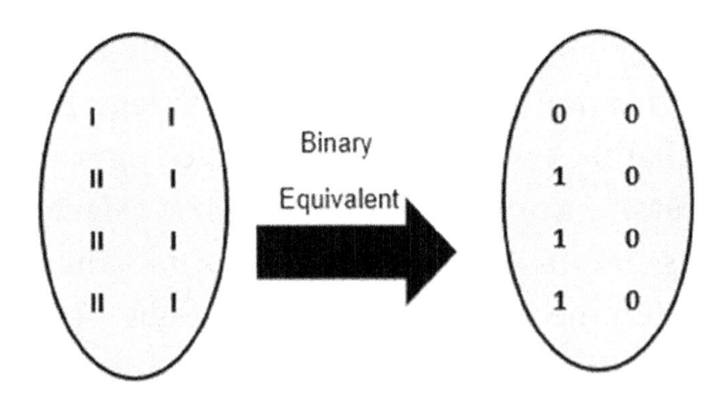

Figure 3. A schematic of Odu Ogbe-Obara's symmetric signature and its binary equivalent

Below is the hierarchical chart of the 16 major chapters of Odu Ifa (Eji or Meji chapters) with their symmetric signatures and their corresponding binary numbers.

I I I I I I I I 1. Eji- Ogbe	II II II II II II II II 2. Oyẹku- Meji	II II I I I I II II 3. Iwori- Meji	I I II II II II I I 4. Odi- Meji
I I I I II II II II 5. Irosu- Meji	II II II II I I I I 6. Ọwọnrin- Meji	I I II II II II II II 7. Ọbara- Meji	II II II II II II I I 8. Ọkanran- Meji
I I I I I I II II 9. Ogunda- Meji	II II I I I I I I 10. Ọsa- Meji	II II I I II II II II 11. Ika- Meji	II II II II I I II II 12. Oturupọn- Meji
I I II II I I I I 13. Otura- Meji	I I I I II II I I 14. Iretẹ- Meji	I I II II I I II II 15. Ọsẹ- Meji	II II I I II II I I 16. Ofun- Meji

Table 3. The 16 major chapters of Odu Ifa and their symbolic signatures

0 0 0 0 0 0 0 0 1. Eji- Ogbe	1 1 1 1 1 1 1 1 2. Oyẹku- Meji	1 1 0 0 0 0 1 1 13. Iwori- Meji	0 0 1 1 1 1 0 0 4. Odi- Meji
0 0 0 0 1 1 1 1 5. Irosun- Meji	1 1 1 1 0 0 0 0 6. Ọwọnrin- Meji	0 0 1 1 1 1 1 1 7. Ọbara- Meji	1 1 1 1 1 1 0 0 8. Ọkanran- Meji
0 0 0 0 0 0 1 1 9. Ogunda- Meji	1 1 0 0 0 0 0 0 10. Ọsa- Meji	1 1 0 0 1 1 1 1 11. Ika- Meji	1 1 1 1 0 0 1 1 12. Oturupọn- Meji
0 0 1 1 0 0 0 0 13. Otura- Meji	0 0 0 0 1 1 0 0 14. Iretẹ- Meji	0 0 1 1 0 0 1 1 15. Ọsẹ- Meji	1 1 0 0 1 1 0 0 16. Ofun- Meji

Table 4. The 16 major chapters of Odu Ifa and their equivalent binary signatures

Chapter Four

The order of seniority of Odu Ifa in the Odu Ifa corpus

The order of seniority of Odu Ifa is very important because it is this order that establishes the parameters of information retrieval in the Ifa knowledge base. The order of seniority varies from one region to another in Yorubaland. Accordingly, the order that is described in this chapter is the most common one in many Yoruba communities.

As I have mentioned in chapter three, to simplify the Odu Ifa hierarchy, the Ifa literary corpus can be organized into 16 books with 256 different chapters. The 256 chapters can further be sub-divided into 16 major chapters and 240 minor chapters. Each book in the Ifa literary corpus has one major chapter and more than one minor chapter except for the book of Ofun that has one major chapter (Ofun-Meji) and no minor chapter.

The first book, in the Ifa literary corpus, is Ogbe. The book of Ogbe has 31 chapters. The 31 chapters, in descending order of rank or seniority, are:

1. Eji-Ogbe
2. Ogbe-Ọyẹku
3. Ogbe-Iwori
4. Ogbe-Odi
5. Ogbe-Irosun
6. Ogbe-Ọwọnrin
7. Ogbe-Ọbara
8. Ogbe-Ọkanran
9. Ogbe-Ogunda
10. Ogbe-Ọsa
11. Ogbe-Ika
12. Ogbe-Oturupọn
13. Ogbe-Otura
14. Ogbe-Irẹtẹ
15. Ogbe-Ọsẹ
16. Ogbe-Ofun
17. Ọyẹku-Ogbe
18. Iwori-Ogbe
19. Odi-Ogbe
20. Irosun-Ogbe
21. Ọwọnrin-Ogbe
22. Ọbara-Ogbe
23. Ọkanran-Ogbe
24. Ogunda-Ogbe
25. Ọsa-Ogbe
26. Ika-Ogbe
27. Oturupọn-Ogbe
28. Otura-Ogbe
29. Irẹtẹ-Ogbe
30. Ọsẹ-Ogbe
31. Ofun-Ogbe

Accordingly, the highest-ranked chapter in the book of Ogbe is Eji-Ogbe or Ogbe-Meji (a major chapter). Eji-Ogbe is also the highest-ranked chapter among the 16 major chapters in the Ifa literary corpus. In fact, Eji-Ogbe outranks every other chapter in all 16 books in the Ifa literary corpus.

The second book, in the Odu Ifa literary corpus, is Ọyẹku. The book of Ọyẹku comprises 29 chapters. The 29 chapters, in descending order of rank or seniority, are:

1. Ọyẹku-Meji
2. Ọyẹku-Iwori
3. Ọyẹku-Odi
4. Ọyẹku-Irosun
5. Ọyẹku-Ọwọnrin
6. Ọyẹku-Ọbara
7. Ọyẹku-Ọkanran
8. Ọyẹku-Ogunda
9. Ọyẹku-Ọsa
10. Ọyẹku-Ika
11. Ọyẹku-Oturupọn
12. Ọyẹku-Otura
13. Ọyẹku-Irẹtẹ
14. Ọyẹku-Ọsẹ
15. Ọyẹku-Ofun
16. Iwori-Ọyẹku
17. Odi-Ọyẹku
18. Irosun-Ọyẹku
19. Ọwọnrin-Ọyẹku
20. Ọbara-Ọyẹku
21. Ọkanran-Ọyẹku
22. Ogunda-Ọyẹku
23. Ọsa-Ọyẹku
24. Ika-Ọyẹku
25. Oturupọn-Ọyẹku
26. Otura-Ọyẹku
27. Irẹtẹ-Ọyẹku
28. Ọsẹ-Ọyẹku
29. Ofun-Ọyẹku

As such, the highest-ranked chapter in the book of Ọyẹku is Ọyẹku-Meji (a major chapter). Ọyẹku-Meji is also the second-ranked major chapter among the 16 major chapters in the Ifa literary corpus.

The third book, in the Odu Ifa literary corpus, is Iwori. The book of Iwori comprises 27 chapters. The 27 chapters, in descending order of rank or seniority, are:

1. Iwori-Meji
2. Iwori-Odi
3. Iwori-Irosun
4. Iwori-Ọwọnrin
5. Iwori-Ọbara
6. Iwori-Ọkanran
7. Iwori-Ogunda
8. Iwori-Ọsa
9. Iwori-Ika
10. Iwori-Oturupọn
11. Iwori-Otura
12. Iwori-Irẹtẹ
13. Iwori-Ọsẹ
14. Iwori-Ofun
15. Odi-Iwori
16. Irosun-Iwori
17. Ọwọnrin-Iwori
18. Ọbara-Iwori
19. Ọkanran-Iwori
20. Ogunda-Iwori
21. Ọsa-Iwori
22. Ika-Iwori
23. Oturupọn-Iwori
24. Otura-Iwori
25. Irẹtẹ-Iwori
26. Ọsẹ-Iwori
27. Ofun-Iwori

Accordingly, the highest-ranked chapter in the book of Iwori is Iwori-Meji (a major chapter). Iwori-Meji is also the third-ranked major chapter among the 16 major chapters in the Ifa literary corpus.

The fourth book, in the Odu Ifa literary corpus, is Odi. The book of Odi comprises 25 chapters. The 25 chapters, in descending order of rank or seniority, are:

1. Odi-Meji
2. Odi-Irosun
3. Odi-Ọwọnrin
4. Odi-Ọbara
5. Odi-Ọkanran
6. Odi-Ogunda
7. Odi-Ọsa
8. Odi-Ika
9. Odi-Oturupọn
10. Odi-Otura
11. Odi-Irẹtẹ
12. Odi-Ọsẹ
13. Odi-Ofun
14. Irosun-Odi
15. Ọwọnrin-Odi
16. Ọbara-Odi
17. Ọkanran-Odi
18. Ogunda-Odi
19. Ọsa-Odi
20. Ika-Odi
21. Oturupọn-Odi
22. Otura-Odi
23. Irẹtẹ-Odi
24. Ọsẹ-Odi
25. Ofun-Odi

The highest-ranked chapter in the book of Odi is Odi-Meji (a major chapter). Odi-Meji is also the fourth-ranked major chapter among the 16 major chapters in the Ifa literary corpus.

The fifth book, in the Odu Ifa literary corpus, is Irosun. The book of Irosun has 23 chapters. The 23 chapters, in descending order of rank or seniority, are:

1. Irosun-Meji
2. Irosun-Ọwọnrin
3. Irosun-Ọbara
4. Irosun-Ọkanran
5. Irosun-Ogunda
6. Irosun-Ọsa
7. Irosun-Ika
8. Irosun-Oturupọn
9. Irosun-Otura
10. Irosun-Irẹtẹ
11. Irosun-Ọsẹ
12. Irosun-Ofun
13. Ọwọnrin-Irosun
14. Ọbara-Irosun
15. Ọkanran-Irosun
16. Ogunda-Irosun
17. Ọsa-Irosun
18. Ika-Irosun
19. Oturupọn-Irosun
20. Otura-Irosun
21. Irẹtẹ-Irosun
22. Ọsẹ-Irosun
23. Ofun-Irosun

Accordingly, the highest-ranked chapter in the book of Irosun is Irosun-Meji (a major chapter). Irosun-Meji is also the fifth-ranked major chapter among the 16 major chapters in the Ifa literary corpus.

The sixth book, in the Odu Ifa literary corpus, is Ọwọnrin. The book of Ọwọnrin comprises 21 chapters. The 21 chapters, in descending order of rank or seniority, are:

1. Ọwọnrin-Meji	8. Ọwọnrin-Otura	15. Ọsa-Ọwọnrin
2. Ọwọnrin-Ọbara	9. Ọwọnrin-Irẹtẹ	16. Ika-Ọwọnrin
3. Ọwọnrin-Ọkanran	10. Ọwọnrin-Ọsẹ	17. Oturupọn-Ọwọnrin
4. Ọwọnrin-Ogunda	11. Ọwọnrin-Ofun	18. Otura-Ọwọnrin
5. Ọwọnrin-Ọsa	12. Ọbara-Ọwọnrin	19. Irẹtẹ-Ọwọnrin
6. Ọwọnrin-Ika	13. Ọkanran-Ọwọnrin	20. Ọsẹ-Ọwọnrin
7. Ọwọnrin-Oturupọn	14. Ogunda-Ọwọnrin	21. Ofun-Ọwọnrin

Accordingly, the highest-ranked chapter in the book of Ọwọnrin is Ọwọnrin-Meji (a major chapter). Ọwọnrin-Meji is also the sixth-ranked major chapter among the 16 major chapters in the Ifa literary corpus.

The seventh book, in the Odu Ifa literary corpus, is Ọbara. The book of Ọbara comprises 19 chapters. The 19 chapters, in descending order of rank or seniority, are:

1. Ọbara-Meji	8. Ọbara-Irẹtẹ	15. Oturupọn-Ọbara
2. Ọbara-Ọkanran	9. Ọbara-Ọsẹ	16. Otura-Ọbara
3. Ọbara-Ogunda	10. Ọbara-Ofun	17. Irẹtẹ-Ọbara
4. Ọbara-Ọsa	11. Ọkanran-Ọbara	18. Ọsẹ-Ọbara
5. Ọbara-Ika	12. Ogunda-Ọbara	19. Ofun-Ọbara
6. Ọbara-Oturupọn	13. Ọsa-Ọbara	
7. Ọbara-Otura	14. Ika-Ọbara	

Accordingly, the highest-ranked chapter in the book of Ọbara is Ọbara-Meji (a major chapter). Ọbara-Meji is also the seventh-ranked major chapter among the 16 major chapters in the Ifa literary corpus.

The eighth book, in the Odu Ifa literary corpus, is Ọkanran. The book of Ọkanran comprises 17 chapters. The 17 chapters, in descending order of rank or seniority, are:

1. Ọkanran-Meji
2. Ọkanran-Ogunda
3. Ọkanran-Ọsa
4. Ọkanran-Ika
5. Ọkanran-Oturupọn
6. Ọkanran-Otura
7. Ọkanran-Irẹtẹ
8. Ọkanran-Ọsẹ
9. Ọkanran-Ofun
10. Ogunda-Ọkanran
11. Ọsa-Ọkanran
12. Ika-Ọkanran
13. Oturupọn-Ọkanran
14. Otura-Ọkanran
15. Irẹtẹ-Ọkanran
16. Ọsẹ-Ọkanran
17. Ofun-Ọkanran

Accordingly, the highest-ranked chapter in the book of Ọkanran is Ọkanran-Meji (a major chapter). Ọkanran-Meji is also the eighth-ranked major chapter among the 16 major chapters in the Ifa literary corpus.

The ninth book, in the Odu Ifa literary corpus, is Ogunda. The book of Ogunda has 15 chapters. The 15 chapters, in descending order of rank or seniority, are:

1. Ogunda-Meji	6. Ogunda-Irẹtẹ	11. Oturupọn-Ogunda
2. Ogunda-Ọsa	7. Ogunda-Ọsẹ	12. Otura-Ogunda
3. Ogunda-Ika	8. Ogunda-Ofun	13. Irẹtẹ-Ogunda
4. Ogunda-Oturupọn	9. Ọsa-Ogunda	14. Ọsẹ-Ogunda
5. Ogunda-Otura	10. Ika-Ogunda	15. Ofun-Ogunda

Accordingly, the highest-ranked chapter in the book of Ogunda is Ogunda-Meji (a major chapter). Ogunda-Meji is also the ninth-ranked major chapter among the 16 major chapters in the Ifa literary corpus.

The 10th book, in the Odu Ifa literary corpus, is Ọsa. The book of Ọsa has 13 chapters. The 13 chapters, in descending order of rank or seniority, are:

1. Ọsa-Meji	6. Ọsa-Ọsẹ	11. Irẹtẹ-Ọsa
2. Ọsa-Ika	7. Ọsa-Ofun	12. Ọsẹ-Ọsa
3. Ọsa-Oturupọn	8. Ika-Ọsa	13. Ofun-Ọsa
4. Ọsa-Otura	9. Oturupọn-Ọsa	
5. Ọsa-Irẹtẹ	10. Otura-Ọsa	

Accordingly, the highest-ranked chapter in the book of Ọsa is Ọsa-Meji (a major chapter). Ọsa-Meji is also the tenth-ranked major chapter among the 16 major chapters in the Ifa literary corpus.

The 11th book, in the Ifa literary corpus, is Ika. The book of Ika has 11 chapters. The 11 chapters, in descending order of rank or seniority, are:

1. Ika-Meji
2. Ika-Oturupọn
3. Ika-Otura
4. Ika-Irẹtẹ
5. Ika-Ọsẹ
6. Ika-Ofun
7. Oturupọn-Ika
8. Otura-Ika
9. Irẹtẹ-Ika
10. Ọsẹ-Ika
11. Ofun-Ika

Accordingly, the highest-ranked chapter in the book of Ika is Ika-Meji (a major chapter). Ika-Meji is also the 12th-ranked major chapter among the 16 major chapters in the Ifa literary corpus.

The 12th book in the Ifa literary corpus is Oturupọn. The book of Oturupọn has 9 chapters. The 9 chapters, in descending order of rank or seniority, are:

1. Oturupọn-Meji
2. Oturupọn-Otura
3. Oturupọn-Irẹtẹ
4. Oturupọn-Ọsẹ
5. Oturupọn-Ofun
6. Otura-Oturupọn
7. Irẹtẹ-Oturupọn
8. Ọsẹ-Oturupọn
9. Ofun-Oturupọn

Accordingly, the highest-ranked chapter in the book of Oturupọn is Oturupọn-Meji (a major chapter). Oturupọn-Meji is also the 12th-ranked major chapter among the 16 major chapters in the Ifa literary corpus.

The 13th book, in the Ifa literary corpus, is Otura. The book of Otura has 7 chapters. The 7 chapters, in descending order of rank or seniority, are:

1. Otura-Meji
2. Otura-Irẹtẹ
3. Otura-Ọsẹ
4. Otura-Ofun
5. Irẹtẹ-Otura
6. Ọsẹ-Otura
7. Ofun-Otura

Accordingly, the highest-ranked chapter in the book of Otura is Otura-Meji (a major chapter). Otura-Meji is also the 13th-ranked major chapter among the 16 major chapters in the Ifa literary corpus.

The 14th book, in the Ifa literary corpus, is Irẹtẹ. The book of Irẹtẹ has 5 chapters. The 5 chapters, in descending order of rank or seniority, are:

1. Irẹtẹ-Meji
2. Irẹtẹ-Ọsẹ
3. Irẹtẹ-Ofun
4. Ọsẹ-Irẹtẹ
5. Ofun-Irẹtẹ

Accordingly, the highest-ranked chapter in the book of Irẹtẹ is Irẹtẹ-Meji (a major chapter). Irẹtẹ-Meji is also the 14th-ranked major chapter among the 16 major chapters in the Ifa literary corpus.

The 15th book, in the Ifa literary corpus, is Ọsẹ. The book of Ọsẹ has 3 chapters. The 3 chapters, in descending order of rank or seniority, are:

1. Ọsẹ-Meji
2. Ọsẹ-Ofun
3. Ofun-Ọsẹ

Accordingly, the highest-ranked chapter in the book of Ọsẹ is Ọsẹ-Meji (a major chapter). Ọsẹ-Meji is also the 15th-ranked major chapter among the 16 major chapters in the Ifa literary corpus.

The 16th book, which is the last book in the Ifa literary corpus, is Ofun. The book of Ofun has only 1 chapter: Ofun-Meji (a major chapter), making it the only book without a minor chapter. Accordingly, since the book of Ofun has only 1 chapter, its highest-ranked chapter is also its only chapter:

1. Ofun-Meji

From the foregoing Odu Ifa hierarchy, one can easily see that each book has two chapters less than the previous one. The reason for this is because some of the minor Odu chapters have already appeared in the previous books, so there is no need to repeat them in the progression. For example, Ogbe-Ọyẹku and Ọyẹku-Ogbe, two minor chapters, have already appeared in book one (the book of Ogbe), so there is no need to repeat them in book two (the book of Ọyẹku). Similarly, Ọyẹku-Iwori and Iwori-Ọyẹku have already appeared in book two, so there is no need to repeat them in book three (the book of Iwori).

Part of understanding the Odu Ifa hierarchy is the mastery of the structure of the two legs of Ifa and the position of each leg in the Odu Ifa hierarchical chart. This provides a shortcut methodology for determining the seniority of each Odu during the process of divination without having to recite all the 256 Odu to make this determination. At first glance, the methodology might seem difficult, but there is an underlying simplicity to it that will become evident as we proceed.

Generally, when two Odu are cast, seniority is determined based on the rank of the right leg of each Odu. For example, if Ọyẹku-Ọbara (a minor Odu) and Ọkanran-Odi (a minor Odu) were to emerge from the first and second castings respectively, Ọyẹku-Ọbara would be indicated as the senior because the right leg of Ọyẹku-Ọbara (Ọyẹku) ranks higher on the Odu Ifa hierarchical chart than the right leg of Ọkanran-Odi (Ọkanran).

L	R	L	R
I	II	I	II
II	II	II	II
II	II	II	II
II	II	I	I
Ọyẹku-Ọbara		Ọkanran-Odi	

There are a few exceptions to the general rule. For example, if the first and second castings generate two minor Odu respectively, which have the same right legs and different left legs, say Ọbara-Ọyẹku and Ọbara-Iwori, seniority is determined based on the rank of the left leg of each Odu.

L	R	L	R
II	I	II	I
II	II	I	II
II	II	I	II
II	II	II	II
Ọbara-Ọyẹku		Ọbara-Iwori	

In this case, Ọbara-Ọyẹku is the senior of the two emergent Odu because Ọyẹku, which is the left leg of Odu Ọbara-Ọyẹku, ranks higher than Iwori, the left leg of Odu Ọbara-Iwori. In addition, if a major Odu and a minor Odu emerge in the first and second castings respectively, the major Odu would be indicated as the senior because every major Odu outranks every minor Odu on the Odu Ifa hierarchical chart. Lastly, if Ogbe-Meji (aka Eji-Ogbe) or Ofun-Meji emerges from the first casting, there is no need for any other casting because Ogbe-Meji is the king and the leader of all the Odu in the Ifa corpus while Ofun-Meji is the eldest of the Odu. This explains why Ogbe-Meji is the highest-ranked major chapter of Odu Ifa and why Ofun-Meji, in spite of its low position, on the Odu Ifa hierarchical chart, is ranked just as high as Ogbe-Meji.

Chapter Five

Ifa divination: process and practice

There are different divinatory instruments that are used in the process of Ifa divination across Yoruba-land. However, in this chapter, I will limit my discussion to four major divinatory instruments: the Ikin, Ọpẹlẹ, Ọpọn Ifa and ibo. Below is a brief description of each of the four major divinatory instruments.

The Ikin (The 16 Sacred Palm Nuts)

The Ikin is believed to be the first and the most ancient of the divinatory instruments. The Ikin is a collection of 16 sacred palm nuts (ekurọ), each of which usually has four or more eyelets. The sacred palm nuts come from the palm oil tree (ọpẹ), which usually grows in a tropical environment. According to Bascom (1969):

> The oil palm (ọpẹ) or Elaeis guineensis bears fruit (ẹyin) in large bunches (idi ẹyin, banga); each fruit consists of a palm nut covered with a reddish-orange pericarp from which palm oil (epo) is extracted for cooking and for export. The nuts (ekurọ) themselves are about an inch long, ovoid or egg-shaped, with hard black shells marked with lengthwise grooves. (p. 26).

Figure 4. The Ikin (16 Sacred Palm Nuts in a wooden bowl).

Photo provided by Nathan Lugo.

The Ọpẹlẹ (The Divining Quantum Chain)

The Ọpẹlẹ is a 4x2 quantum chain used in the process of Ifa divination. It is about three-to-four feet long, and it consists of eight halves of seed shells or pods, which are arranged in a 4x2 matrix structure (four rows and two columns) and conjoined by a string with distinguishing studs at both of its two ends. Each half seed shell or pod has two sides, which are concave and convex. Depending on the region, in place of half-seed shells or pods, other objects are used, such as coins, nuts, tokens or any portable objects with two distinct sides. Collectively, I refer to these objects as tokens.

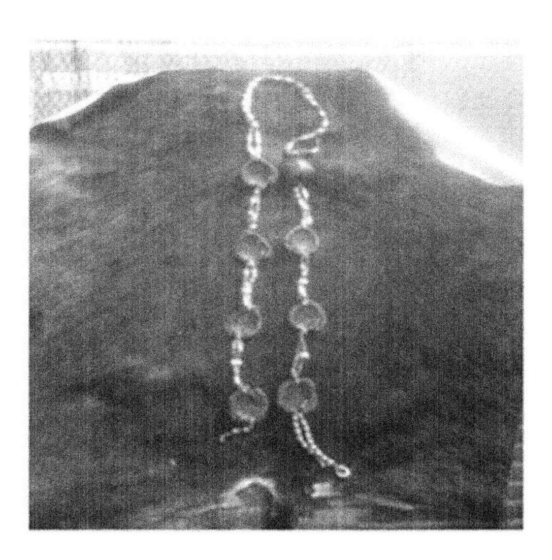

Figure 5. The Ọpẹlẹ quantum chain with its eight half-seed shells, pods or tokens.

Photo provided by Akomolafe Wande.

The Ọpọn Ifa (The Divining Tray)

The Ọpọn Ifa is the divining tray used when performing divination with the Ikin. It varies in shape, but the circular shape is the most common. It is flat and generally made of wood. Its flat surface, as we can see in the figure below, is normally covered with yellow powder (Iyẹrosun) for the diviner to make imprints. Carved in relief around the border of the Ọpọn Ifa are different symbols and anthropomorphic figures associated with divination and Yoruba deities. The top part of the tray is adorned with the face of Ẹṣu, who is the Yoruba deity of justice, the metaphysical governor of the crossroad and the messenger between other deities and the people. In addition, some trays have more than one Ẹṣu face carved in relief around their borders.

Figure 6. The divining tray.

Photo provided by Akomolafe Wande.

The Ibo Objects

The ibo objects, as a collective, form an important instrument for casting lots. Generally, the ibo are used by the Babalawo to translate the message as contained in the emergent ẹsẹ Ifa into concrete or specific details. There are different ibo objects, but the most commonly used are the cowries and the bones. Each set of ibo objects symbolize different things and notions. For example, the cowries symbolize ire (good or fortune) or affirmative (yes); whereas, the bones symbolize ibi (evil or misfortune) or negative (no). The action word "bo" in the Yoruba language simply means "to cover" or "to hide." Ibo, therefore, literally means an object for covering something, which alludes to the closed or secret ibo technique described below, in the topic about the process of Ifa divination.

Figure 7. An ibo object.

Photo provided by Onanuga Ololade.

The process of Ifa divination

The process of Ifa divination usually starts with an inquiry made by the client, who may be an individual, a family group, or an entire community. The individual client consults the Babalawo mostly when he or she needs clarity, insight and guidance in making a very important decision. There is always the unknown, which presumably is known to Ifa through the process of divination. "This condition of uncertainty, which is always present in the human experience, is what invites the visit to Ifa to take care of all possibilities" (Olupona and Abiodun, 2016, p. 110). In consonance with the general view, the Yoruba often say, "b'onii ti ri ọla o ri bẹẹ, lo n mu Babalawo d'ifa ọrọọrun;" meaning, the dynamic nature of reality is what necessitates periodic divination.

The Babalawo begins the process of divination by paying respect to Olodumare (the Yoruba Godhead), Ọrunmila, the mother earth (Ilẹ), Eṣu, and other Yoruba Oriṣa. The Babalawo, having completed his initial rites of homage, hands one of the divinatory instruments (Ikin or Ọpẹlẹ) to the client to make a silent request of what he or she wants from Ifa. In most cases, the client's inquiry is framed in terms of two mutually exclusive alternative propositions. In other words, the inquiry may be posed to Ifa in terms of two statements, the first affirmative and the second negative, such as: "the decision I am about to make will bring me fortune (Ire)," or "the decision I am about to make will bring me misfortune (Ibi)" (Bascom, 1969, p. 51).

The process of Ifa divination adapts the probability of numbers to model the complexity or the stochastic nature of the human thought process; it narrows every thought to binary choices (i.e. ibi and ire) and produces information that helps the client make the right decision. In the process of Ifa divination, if the Babalawo chooses to use the Ikin as his instrument of divination, he proceeds to generate eight random numbers in eight successive iterations by manipulating the 16 Ikin palm nuts between his left and right hands. The Babalawo puts all the 16 Ikin palm nuts in his left hand and attempts to scoop them all, at once, with his right hand. If, after his first attempt, one Ikin palm nut remains in his left hand, then he marks **II** in the yellow powder on the divining tray. However, if two Ikin palm nuts remain in his left hand, then he marks **I.** If zero or any number of Ikin nuts greater than two is left in the left hand, then no mark is made on the divining tray. The process and the markings progress, eight times, as in the order indicated in figure 8 as A, until a 4x2 signature matrix emerges as depicted in step 8 of B.

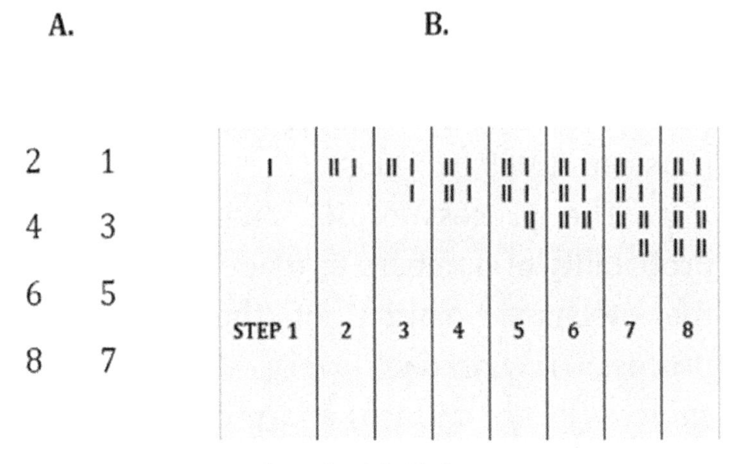

Figure 8. Marking the Odu Ifa figures

The emergent 4x2 signature or pattern above corresponds to one of the 256 chapters of Odu Ifa. In this case, the 4x2 signature matrix corresponds to Odu Irosun-Ọyẹku (11111100=8 bits, reading from right to left). Odu Irosun-Ọyẹku, like the rest of the remaining 255 chapters of Odu Ifa, is a repository of information on ethics, myths, cosmology, philosophy and wisdom. The answer to the client's inquiry will be found only in the emergent Odu. The Babalawo then recites and interprets the information stored in Irosun-Ọyẹku, which will illuminate the nature of the client's predicament and provide the client with the necessary guidance to make the right decision and judgment.

However, if the Babalawo chooses to use the Ọpẹlẹ quantum chain as his instrument of divination, he proceeds to cast the Ọpẹlẹ quantum chain on the ground. And unlike the divination through Ikin that goes through eight iterations to generate a 4x2 signature matrix (see figure 8 above), the Ọpẹlẹ, due to its inherent 4x2 matrix structure, can generate a 4x2 signature matrix in one casting. This makes the Ọpẹlẹ a faster divinatory instrument than the Ikin (see the structure of the Ọpẹlẹ quantum chain in figure 5 above).

When the Babalawo casts the Ọpẹlẹ, if the four tokens on the left column are facing down as the four tokens on the right, the Babalawo will record the emergent binary pattern as:

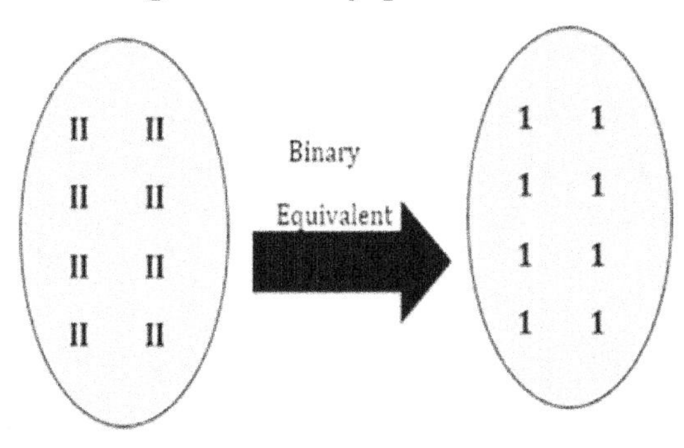

Figure 9. The 4x2 matrix structure of the emergent Odu Ọyẹku-Meji and its binary equivalent

In this scenario, the emergent 4x2 signature matrix or pattern corresponds to Odu Ọyẹku-Meji (11111111=8 bits, reading from right to left). As in the divination through Ikin, the answer to the client's inquiry will be found only in the emergent binary pattern (Ọyẹku-Meji). The Babalawo then proceeds to recite and interpret the information stored in the emergent Odu Ọyẹku-Meji, which will illuminate the nature of the client's predicament and provide the client with the necessary guidance for the right decision and judgment.

In the process of Ifa divination, while the Ikin and the Ọpẹlẹ are generally used for generating the Odu Ifa signatures, the ibo objects are employed for interpreting the message as contained in the pertinent verse of the emergent Odu Ifa. The message as contained in the pertinent verse of the emergent Odu Ifa is usually very broad and generic, thus the ibo objects are employed as a means to narrow down this message to a specific point. There are two main types of ibo techniques: the open ibo technique and the closed ibo technique.

In the open ibo technique, the ibo objects (cowry shells and bones) are revealed to the Babalawo. For instance, if after the first performance of divination with the Ọpẹlẹ, the oracular message as contained in the pertinent verse of the emergent Odu Ifa says the client is going to embark on a journey to a distant land, the client might use the set of ibo to find out specifically the outcome of the predicted journey; that is, is the journey going to bring ire (positive outcome) or ibi (negative outcome)?

Right before casting the Ọpẹlẹ on the ground, the Babalawo touches the Ọpẹlẹ with cowry shells (ibo objects); indicating "ire," and places them on his right side. He then proceeds to touch the Ọpẹlẹ with a piece of bone or another ibo object; indicating "ibi," and places it on his left side. The Babalawo then takes up the Ọpẹlẹ again and casts it on the ground twice. It suffices to mention that the seniority of the emergent Odu Ifa will determine if the ibo on the left side will be picked or the one on the right side. This is why it is very important for the Babalawo to master the order of seniority of each Odu in the Odu Ifa hierarchical chart; particularly, the order of seniority of the 16 major Odu Ifa. So, if, in the first casting, say Odu Ọyẹku-Meji (a second-ranked major Odu) is generated and in the second casting, Odu Ika-Meji (an 11th-ranked major Odu) is generated, then since Odu Ọyẹku-Meji is ranked higher than Odu Ika-Meji in the Odu Ifa hierarchical chart, the ibo on the right side, which indicates ire or affirmative, will be picked and vice versa.

In another example, if in the first casting, Odu Ọyẹku-Ogbe (a minor Odu) is generated and in the second casting, Odu Ogbe-Ọyẹku, another minor Odu, is generated, then since Ọyẹku-Ogbe is ranked lower in the Odu Ifa hierarchical chart than Ogbe-Ọyẹku, the ibo on the left side, which indicates negative or ibi, will be picked and vice versa. Lastly, if in the first casting, Odu Ika-Ogbe (a minor Odu) is generated and in the second casting, another minor Odu Ifa, say Odu Ika-Ọyẹku, is generated, then since the two minor Odu Ifa have the same right leg (Ika) and since Ogbe (the left leg of the first minor Odu) is ranked higher than Ọyẹku (the left leg of the second minor Odu), the ibo on the right side, which indicates affirmative or ire, will be picked and vice versa.

As previously mentioned in chapter four, the general rule is this: if during the two castings, a major Odu Ifa emerges before a minor Odu Ifa, the ibo on the right side, which indicates affirmative or ire, is picked. Otherwise, the ibo on the left side, which indicates negative or ibi, is picked. In addition, if either Odu Eji-Ogbe or Ofun-Meji emerges in the first casting, no more casting is required. The casting stops. The ibo on the right, indicating strong affirmative or ire, is automatically picked. This is because it is generally believed that Eji-Ogbe (also Ogbe-Meji) is the king and the leader of all the Odu in the Ifa corpus while Ofun-Meji is the eldest of the Odu.

The second ibo technique is the closed ibo technique. In his essay, in honor of Professor Wande Abimbola titled *Ifa Divination Process,* Bade Ajayi likens the closed ibo technique to a secret ballot in an election. Unlike the open ibo technique, where the ibo objects are situated openly on both sides of the Babalawo—that is, the cowries on the right side and the bone on the left side, the ibo objects in the closed ibo technique are concealed from the Babalawo. So, right before casting, the Babalawo asks the client to conceal the pair of ibo objects, one in each of their hands. The process of divination then proceeds as in the open ibo technique except, for now, the right hand of the client is the left side of the Babalawo and the left hand of the client is the right side of the Babalawo. This reversal simply has to do with the fact that the client, holding the ibo objects, sits facing the Babalawo. If the emergent Odu Ifa during the first casting of the Ọpẹlẹ is senior to the emergent Odu Ifa during the second casting, the Babalawo will ask his client to reveal the ibo object in their left hand. However, if it is not, the Babalawo will ask his client to reveal the ibo object in their right hand instead. Furthermore, if the ibo object kept in the left hand turns out to be a piece of bone, it means that the answer to the client's question is a negative "no" or ibi. But if it turns out to be a pair of cowries, it means the answer is a strong affirmative "yes" or ire.

In conclusion, during the divination process, the message that the Babalawo shares with his client is obtained directly from the pertinent verses in the emergent Odu Ifa. And as previously mentioned, if this message is too broad, the Babalawo may have to cast the Ọpẹlẹ many times when using the ibo to find out a pertinent answer to the client's inquiry. The general outline, therefore, of the procedure in divination is as follows: first, a cast is made to generate a signature and determine the chapter of Odu Ifa from which the verses are to be recited. Second, two casts are made to narrow down the message from the first cast and determine whether the message from the first cast is for ire or ibi. Third, a succession of casts is made to determine the kind of ire or ibi that is indicated. Fourth, a succession of casts is made to determine if a sacrifice is needed, what kind of sacrifice is required and to whom the sacrifice is to be made. The process varies from one region of Yorubaland to another.

Divination through Ikin is the oldest practice of ifa divination. However, divination through Ọpẹlẹ is a later invention. Some Babalawo prefer to use the Ikin to the Ọpẹlẹ because they believe the Ikin is more accurate than the Ọpẹlẹ. However, other Babalawo prefer the Ọpẹlẹ because they believe the Ọpẹlẹ is faster and less cumbersome than the

Ikin. The Ikin can be likened to a digital computer system because it operates based on the Boolean rule of 0 and 1. However, the Ọpẹlẹ can be likened to a quantum computer system because it operates based on the fundamental principles of quantum mechanics. Both the Ikin and the Ọpẹlẹ operate as an 8-bit pseudo-random number generator.

Chapter Six

Number systems in Ifa divination

The Ifa divination system uses well-known traditional number systems in its operations—that is, the Ifa divination system organizes and manipulates data in its knowledge base, and retrieves data from its knowledge base using traditional number systems. Understanding these number systems is fundamental to understanding how the Ifa divination system operates. Below are the two number systems that we find in the Ifa divination system:

1. Binary number system
2. Hexadecimal number system

Binary number system

The binary number system is a number system that expresses any number as a sum of powers of 2 (i.e. 2^0, 2^1, 2^2, 2^3, 2^4....2^n), and denotes it as a sequence of only two characters: 0 and 1. The binary number system is also called the base-2 number system. Unlike the decimal number system, which progresses from zero, one and the successive numbers up to nine inclusively (i.e. 0, 1, 2, 3, 4, 5, 6, 7, 9), the binary number system only progresses from zero to one (0, 1).

Binary number system in Ifa divination

The Ifa divination system uses binary symbols in its divination technique: one vertical line (I) and two vertical lines (II). The two symbols are based on the complementary dualism of tibi tire, and they can be arranged as a 4x2 matrix of octagrams that can take 2^8 = 256 different values. Each of the 256 octagrams can further be rearranged in a format that resembles modern binary numbers by reading along the right column to the left column, from top to bottom, with one vertical line I as 0 and two vertical lines II as 1. To illustrate this point, let us look at Odu Ọbara-Meji, which is one of the 256 octagrams in the Ifa divination system. Structurally, Ọbara-Meji is represented as:

L	R
I	I
II	II
II	II
II	II

Reading along the right column to the left column, from top to bottom, with one vertical line I as 0 and two vertical lines II as 1, the 4x2 matrix structure of Odu Ọbara-Meji can be rearranged in a format that resembles modern binary numbers 11101110. The remaining 255 octagrams in the Ifa divination system can be rearranged in a similar manner and the relationship between Odu Ifa symbols, binary and decimal numbers is given below.

I I I I I I I I	00000000	0
I I I I I I I II	00000001	1
I I I I I I II I	00000010	2
I I I I I I II II	00000011	3
I I I I I II I I	00000100	4
I I I I I II I II	00000101	5
I I I I I II II I	00000110	6
I I I I I II II II	00000111	7
	-	
	-	
	-	
	-	
II II II II II II II II	11111111	255

Extending the scope of the binary number system

The scope of the binary number system in the Ifa divination can be extended to include exponentiation. Exponentiation or repeated multiplication is the mathematical operation of raising one number to another. It is usually represented in the form: n^x. The number n is called base, and the number x is called exponent. For instance, exponentiation in the base 2 number system is of the form: 2^x. That is to say, the base is 2 and the exponent x can be any integer.

As a base 2 system, the Ifa divination system shows a propensity for number 2. For instance, the Ọpẹlẹ quantum chain operates based on the repeated multiplication of number 2—that is, 2, 4, 8, 16..... $2^8 = 256$. In fact, the operation of the Ọpẹlẹ quantum chain can be represented by a simple exponential function: $f(x) = 2^x$ (where $0 \leq x \leq 8$). Needless to say, x is the number of qutokens on the Ọpẹlẹ quantum chain.

Hexadecimal number system

The hexadecimal number system, also called base-16 or sometimes hex, is a number system that uses 16 unique characters with a combination of digits from 0 through 9 and letters from A through F to represent the decimal numbers 0 through 15. In other words, the decimal numbers 0 through 9 are still used as in the original decimal system, but the decimal numbers 10 through 15 are now represented by capital letters of the alphabet from A through F.

Hexadecimal is also a compact way to express long binary strings (0's and 1's) in modern computers in which a byte is almost always defined as containing eight binary digits. It suffices to know that one hexadecimal digit is equivalent to four binary bits or a half-byte. So, two hexadecimal digits correspond to eight binary bits or one byte: two hex digits = 1 byte. In other words, with two hexadecimal digits, we can express any number from 0 through 255. To do the same in binary, we need 8 digits. For example, binary 0101 1111, which is one byte, corresponds to 5F in hexadecimal—that is, binary 0101 = hex 5 and binary 1111 = hex F. As we can see, by splitting 8 binary bits into two groups of 4 bits and by representing each group of 4 bits by one hexadecimal value, we can represent large binary strings with much fewer digits. Also, since a byte may take $2^8 = 256$ different values, we can express any of these values with different combinations of two hexadecimal digits, ranging from 00 to FF. To do the same in binary, we need 8 binary digits.

Hexadecimal number system in Ifa divination

The Ifa divination system uses hexadecimal digits in its organization of information and in its divination technique. The convenient method of data management in the Ifa divination system is by organizing the Ifa literary corpus into a set of 16 books with 256 different chapters. As I have previously mentioned in chapters two and three, the Ifa literary corpus has its unique signature or identifier. Thus, since $16 = 2^4$, then 4 binary digits are required to address or identify each of the 16 books that constitute the Ifa literary corpus. The 16 books that constitute the Ifa literary corpus and their corresponding signatures or identifiers are: Ogbe (I I I I), Ọyẹku (II II II II), Iwori (II I I II), Odi (I II II I), Irosun (II II I I), Ọwọnrin (I I II II), Ọbara (II II II I), Ọkanran (I II II II), Ogunda (II I I I), Ọsa (I I I II), Ika (II II I II), Oturupọn (II I II II), Otura (I I II I), Irẹtẹ (I II I I), Ọsẹ (II I II I) and Ofun (I II I II). Thus, the 4-bit signature of each book in the Odu Ifa literary corpus is one hexadecimal digit. In other words, the 4-bit signature of each book in the Odu Ifa literary corpus can be referred to as the Ifa-hex signature. The relationship between Ifa-hex signature, standard binary value and hexadecimal is given as:

The 16 books in the Ifa corpus	Ifa-hex signature	Standard binary value	Hexa-decimal value
Ogbe	I I I I	0000	0
Ọyẹku	II II II II	1111	F
Iwori	II I I II	1001	9
Odi	I II II I	0110	6
Irosun	II II I I	1100	C
Ọwọnrin	I I II II	0011	3
Ọbara	II II II I	1110	E
Ọkanran	I II II II	0111	7
Ogunda	II I I I	1000	8
Ọsa	I I I II	0001	1
Ika	II II I II	1101	D
Oturupọn	II I II II	1011	B
Otura	I I II I	0010	2
Irẹtẹ	I II I I	0100	4
Ọsẹ	II I II I	1010	A
Ofun	I II I II	0101	5

Additionally, since $256 = 2^8$, then 8 binary bits are required to identify each of the 256 chapters that constitutes the Ifa literary corpus. While there are 256 chapters in the Ifa literary corpus, these chapters are divided into two groups: 16 major chapters and 240 minor chapters. Here is a list of the 16 major chapters in the Ifa literary corpus and their corresponding symmetric 8-bit signatures: Eji-Ogbe or Ogbe-Meji (I I I I I I I I), Ọyẹku-Meji (II II II II II II II II), Iwori-Meji (II I I II II I I II), Odi-Meji (I II II I I II II I), Irosun-Meji (II II I I II II I I), Ọwọnrin-Meji (I I II II I I II II), Ọbara-Meji (II II II I II II II I), Ọkanran-Meji (I II II II I II II II), Ogunda-Meji (II I I I II I I I), Ọsa-Meji (I I I II I I I II), Ika-

Meji (II II I II II II I II), Oturupọn-Meji (II I II II II I II II), Otura-Meji (I I II I I I II I), Irẹtẹ-Meji (I II I I I II I I), Ọsẹ-Meji (II I II I II I II I) and Ofun-Meji (I II I II I II I II). Eji or Meji, in Yoruba language, simply means two, which explains why the signature of each major chapter of Odu Ifa, as depicted above, consists of two identical 4-bit halves—that is, Ọyẹku-Meji (two identical Ọyẹku - II II II II II II II II), Iwori-Meji (two identical Iwori - II I I II II I I II), etc. Thus, the 8-bit signature of each chapter in the Odu Ifa literary corpus is two hexadecimal digits. The relationship between Odu Ifa signature, standard binary value and hexadecimal value is given below.

The 16 major Odu-Ifa chapters	8-bit Odu-Ifa Signature	Standard binary value	Hexa-decimal value
Ogbe-Meji	I I I I I I I I	0000 0000	00
Ọyẹku-Meji	II II II II II II II II	1111 1111	FF
Iwori-Meji	II I I II II I I II	1001 1001	99
Odi-Meji	I II II I I II II I	0110 0110	66
Irosun-Meji	II II I I II II I I	1100 1100	CC
Ọwọnrin-Meji	I I II II I I II II	0011 0011	33
Ọbara-Meji	II II II I II II II I	1110 1110	EE
Ọkanran-Meji	I II II II I II II II	0111 0111	77
Ogunda-Meji	II I I I II I I I	1000 1000	88
Ọsa-Meji	I I I II I I I II	0001 0001	11
Ika-Meji	II II I II II II I II	1101 1101	DD
Oturupọn-Meji	II I II II II I II II	1011 1011	BB
Otura-Meji	I I II I I I II I	0010 0010	22
Irẹtẹ-Meji	I II I I I II I I	0100 0100	44
Ọsẹ-Meji	II I II I II I II I	1010 1010	AA
Ofun-Meji	I II I II I II I II	0101 0101	55

Chapter Seven

Ifa divination system and its convergence with digital computer systems

The huge amount of scholarly literature that has been generated about Ifa and its divination system is notably weak on some of the elements of technological knowledge that are embedded in the Ifa divination system; especially, the convergence of Ifa divination system and digital computer systems. I must say that anyone who has taken the time to study the structure and the operational mechanics of Ifa divination system, from a technological perspective, would recognize that the Ifa divination system is a form of an indigenous computer system.

For instance, the Ifa divination system, like a modern digital computer, uses binary notation and logic in its operation. In fact, some scholars (Eglash et al) are of the view that the binary code theory, which is the base for Boolean algebra and modern computer systems, has its origin in the binary concept of the Ifa divination system. In addition, the Ifa divination system, just like a modern digital computer, was developed to store, process and retrieve information.

It is my goal, in this chapter, to use the operational mechanics of the divinatory instrument of Ikin and the structure of Odu Ifa to show the similarities between the Ifa divination system and digital computer systems.

What is a digital computer system?

A digital computer system is a device that is designed to store, process and output information in a digital format—that is, a digital computer manipulates information in digital, or more precisely, binary form. A binary number, as I have previously mentioned in chapter six, has only two discrete values: zero and one. Each of these discrete values is represented by the OFF and ON status of an electronic switch called a transistor. Thus, all digital computers only understand binary numbers.

A digital computer must have mechanisms for input, storage, processing and output—that is, a digital computer takes in raw data or information via its input unit or interface, stores it in memory until it is ready to work on it, manipulates it with its processor, and then communicates the results to the user via its output interface. So, all the main parts of a computer system can be divided into one of these four units:

- **Input unit:** this is the interface through which information gets into the computer. Computer keyboards, mouse and microphones are examples of input units.
- **Memory:** this is where the information can be stored and retrieved. In the most general sense, memory can refer to external storage such as disk drives or tape drives. However, in common usage, it refers only to a computer's main memory, the fast semiconductor storage (RAM) directly connected to the processor.
- **Processor or the central processing unit (CPU):** this is the computational and control unit of a computer. The CPU is the device

that interprets and executes information or instructions. The CPU is often called the brain of a computer because of its ability to fetch, decode and execute instructions and to transfer information to and from other resources over the computer's main data-transfer path.

- **Output unit:** this is the interface through which the results of processed information are communicated or displayed to the user.

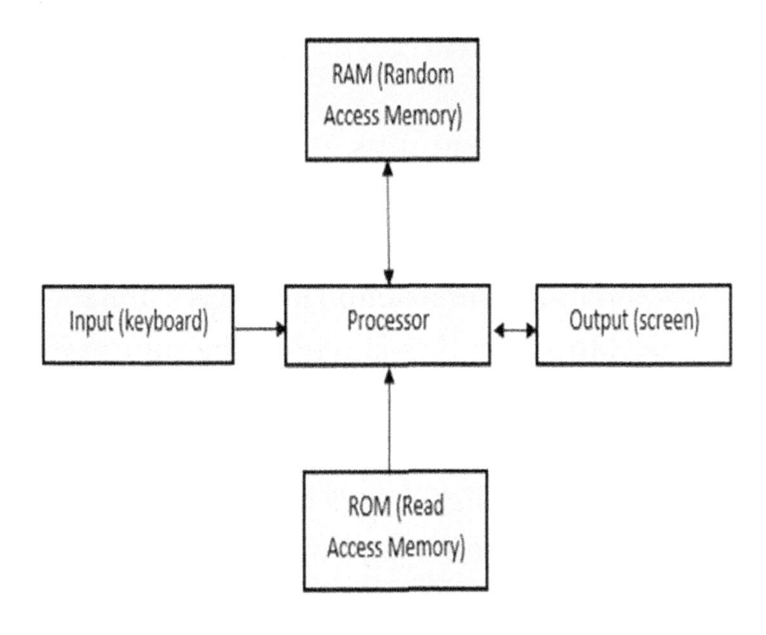

Figure 10. A block diagram of the four components of a digital computer

Explanation of basic terms associated with digital computers

- **Bit (short for binary digit):** is the smallest unit of data or information handled by a computer. One bit expresses a 1 or a 0 in a binary numeral, or a true or false logical condition, and is represented physically by an element such as a high or a low voltage at one point in an electrical circuit. A single bit conveys little information that we would consider meaningful. However, a group of 8 bits makes up a byte, which is equivalent to one alphanumeric character, which is a letter of the alphabet, a decimal digit, or some other character. So, all the information that digital computers process and instructions they execute are made up of a group of bits.
- **Byte (short for binary term):** is a unit of data, almost always consisting of 8 bits and 8 bits = 1 byte. A byte can represent a single character, such as a letter, a digit, or punctuation mark. Since a byte represents only a small amount of information, the amounts of computer memory and storage capacity are usually given in kilobytes (1024 bytes), megabytes (1,048,576 bytes), or gigabytes (1,073,741,824 bytes).

- **Memory address:** is a unique identifier that shows where a piece of information is stored in a computer's memory. The computer's central processing unit (CPU) uses the memory address to track where data and instructions are stored in memory. Structurally, we can imagine the computer memory to be organized as a matrix of bits or as an array of storage boxes, each of which is one byte in length. In this matrix, each row represents a memory location—that is, each row is equal to the word size of the architecture or a group of bytes. For instance, if we have a 16-bit addressable memory, we can organize this memory as 1x16 bits or 2x8 bits. Each row has a natural number address, from 0 to $2^n - 1$, which is used in selecting the row:

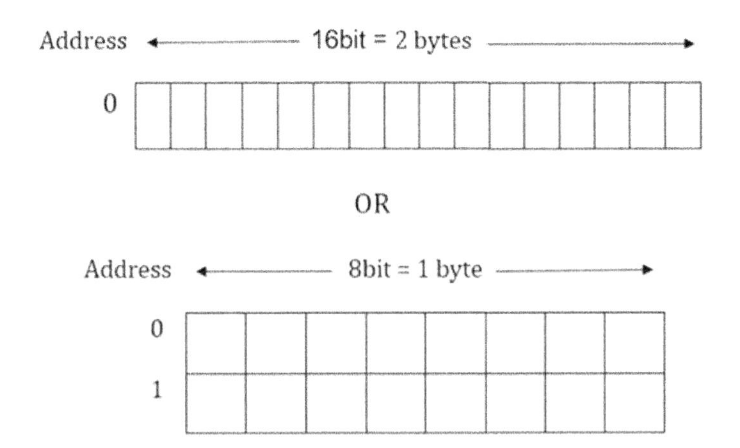

Most modern computer systems have the capacity to store long strings of data. Consequently, memory addresses are represented using hexadecimal numbers because, as previously mentioned in chapter six, hexadecimal number provides a compact way to express long binary strings (0's and 1's) in modern computers in which a byte is almost always defined as containing eight binary digits.

- **ASCII codes (an acronym for American Standard Code for Information Interchange):** is a coding scheme using 7 or 8 bits to assign numeric values to up to 256 characters, including letters, numerals, punctuation marks, control characters and other symbols. The current ASCII standards map all the printable, non-printable and extended characters on your keyboard to numbers. Since computers only understand zeros and ones, every instruction or information that the computer receives has to be converted to binary strings before it can be processed by the computer's CPU. For example, if the computer system receives an instruction to store the two-letter word "go" in memory, the computer would only store the ASCII code of each letter that constitutes this word as a binary string of bits. The ASCII value of lowercase letter g is 103, and its corresponding binary value is 01100111; whereas, the ASCII value of lowercase letter o is 111; its binary value is 01101111. Therefore, the word "go" would be stored as a string of 16 binary digits or 2 bytes (16 bits = 2 bytes)—that is, 01100111 01101111.

The Ikin and digital computer systems

The Ikin is one of the major instruments in the Ifa divination system. It is a collection of 16 sacred palm nuts that can be manipulated logically to construct a 4x2 signature matrix (8 bits). The Ikin, therefore, is generally adapted to generate random 8-bit signatures, which are used to access and retrieve data from the Ifa literary corpus, and communicate data to the client. In terms of operational structure, the Ikin is very similar to a digital computer system. The Ikin, like a digital computer system, has mechanisms for input, storage, logical operations and output.

During the divination process using the Ikin, certain information is whispered or communicated to the Ikin, in form of an inquiry, just as a digital computer takes in raw data or information via its input unit or interface. The diviner would then proceed to manipulate the Ikin sacred palm nuts, generate a random 8-bit signature, use the generated 8-bit signature to access historical data that is stored in memory and communicate the information to the client just as a digital computer uses its CPU to access data in memory, retrieve the necessary information and communicate it to the user.

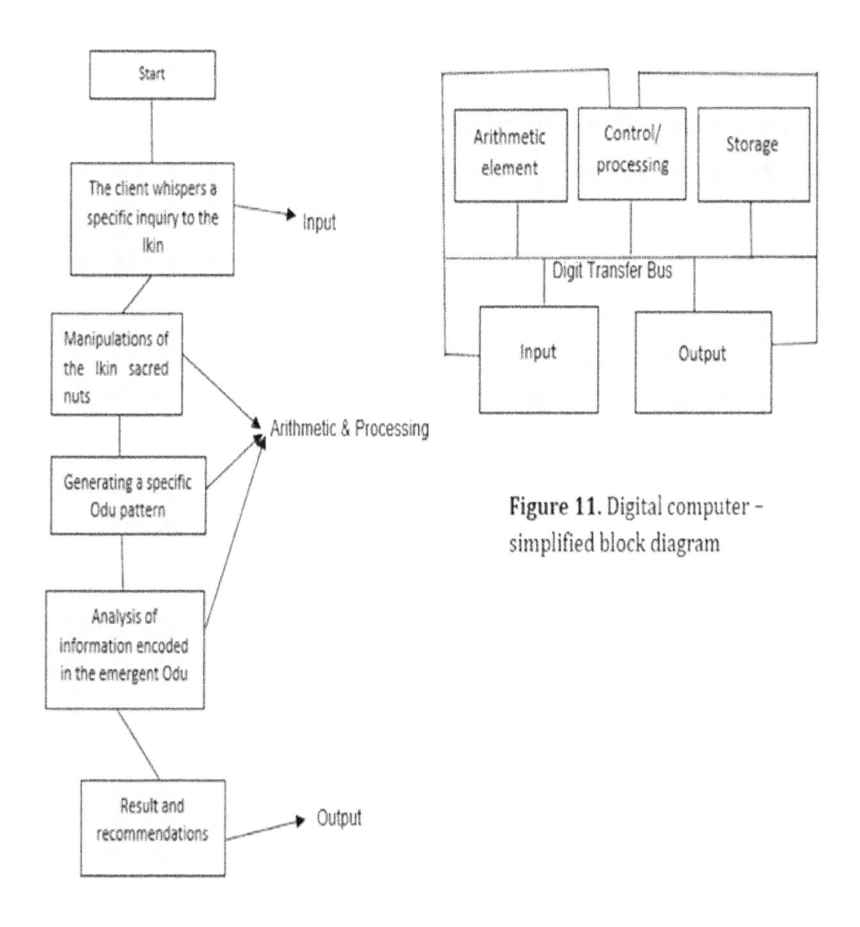

Figure 11. Digital computer - simplified block diagram

Figure 12. A flow chart showing the basic steps in the Ifa divination using the Ikin

Binary operation using the Ikin

The Ikin operates based on the Boolean rule of odd and even binary counts. During the divination process using the Ikin, the 16 Ikin nuts are gathered in the left hand. An attempt is made to scoop, at once, all the 16 Ikin nuts with the right hand. If after the attempt to scoop all 16 Ikin nuts with the right hand, one Ikin nut remains in the left hand, then the binary symbol II is marked on the divination board. However, if two Ikin nuts remain in the left hand, then the binary symbol I is marked on the divination board. If zero or any number of nuts greater than two is left in the left hand, then no mark is made on the divination board. In other words, if letter x represents the total number of nuts that remain in the left hand after an attempt to scoop all 16 nuts with the right hand in one try and $x = 1$, then mark II, which is equivalent to binary number 1. And if $x = 2$, then mark I, which is equivalent to binary number 0. However, if $x < 1$ or $x > 2$, then mark nothing. The process and the markings progress repeatedly, eight times, until a 4x2 signature matrix emerges. For instance, if after an 8-step iteration, the following values of x are obtained: 1,2,2,2,1,2,2,2. The emergent 4x2 asymmetric signature will look like this:

I II

I I

I II

I I

or like this, in binary digits:

0 1

0 0

0 1

0 0

The above 4x2 signature matrix is the signature of Odu Ofun-Ogbe, which is one of the 240 minor chapters of Odu Ifa. Thus, the Ikin can be thought of as an 8-bit digital device, which is capable of generating $2^8 = 256$ addresses to address the 256 chapters of Odu Ifa in memory.

Memory addressing in Ifa divination system using the Ikin

Just like the computer memory, which is organized as a matrix of bits or as an array of storage boxes, the Ifa literary corpus is also organized as a matrix of bits or as an array of books with 256 chapters, each of which is addressable with a 4x2 matrix of bits or 1 byte of addressing signature.

It suffices to know that just as many digital computer systems use byte addressing to access data in memory, the Ifa divination system also uses byte addressing to access information in each chapter of Odu Ifa. Consequently, Odu Ifa's addresses, like computer's memory addresses, can be represented using hexadecimal numbers because, as previously stated, hexadecimal numbers provide a compact way to express long binary strings (0's and 1's). For example, Ogunda-Meji's signature, which is II I I I II I I I or 10001000, can be represented in hexadecimal as 88—that is, 1000 (half-byte) is 8 in hexadecimal, which provides a compact way to express the binary strings 10001000. Table 5 further shows the similarities between the operational structure of the Ikin and a digital computer system.

Ikin	Digital Computer
1. Ikin collects information from the client when the client interfaces and whispers to the Ikin sacred nuts.	Digital computers collect information from the user when the user interfaces with the computer via an input device.
2. As an 8-bit system, the Ikin can address 2^8 = 256 chapters of Odu Ifa in the Odu Ifa corpus. So, the Ikin uses byte addressing.	An 8-bit digital computer system can address 2^8 = 256 memory locations. So, many digital computer systems use byte addressing.
3. An Odu Ifa is a unit of Odu corpus that most commonly consists of 8 bits or 1 byte.	A byte is a unit of digital information that most commonly consists of 8 bits.
4. Ikin is a binary system. It operates based on the Boolean rule of odd and even binary counts. There are 16 Ikin nuts. So, if x is the number of nuts that remain in the left hand after an attempt is made to scoop all the 16 nuts, at once, with the right hand and x = 1, then mark II, which is equivalent to binary number 1. And if x = 2, then mark I, which is equivalent to binary number 0. However, if $x < 1$ or $x > 2$, then mark nothing.	A digital computer system is also a binary system. Its logical operation is based on the manipulation of binary digits – 0 or 1, even or odd, on or off, false or true.
5. There is a clear distinction between the binary identifier (signature) of each chapter of Odu Ifa, in the Ifa knowledge base, and the information stored in each chapter of Odu Ifa.	There is also a clear distinction between the identification of a digital computer's storage register, which is used in the order code, and the information stored in the register.
6. Ikin is a digital system because it carries information in discrete chucks (or quanta). In general, Ikin carries information about the number of nuts in the left hand only in two distinct states: "even" and "odd" - there is no in between.	A digital computer also carries information in discrete chunks (or quanta). Virtually all digital computers carry information in discrete states of zeros and ones.
7. The Odu Ifa's signatures or addresses can be represented using hexadecimal numbers.	The Computer's memory addresses are represented using hexadecimal numbers.

Table 5. Showing the similarities between the Ikin and a digital computer system

Fundamentally, the Ifa divination system and a digital computer operate based on the same binary principle. However, in reality, they operate differently. The Ifa divination system incorporates human consciousness and human memory for the storage, interpretation and transmission of information; whereas, digital computers rely strictly on algorithms and electrical circuits.

Computer ASCII codes and Odu Ifa

Computers are automatic arithmetic engines that operate on the Boolean rule of zeros and ones. However, since humans mostly write in words (emails, letters, text messages etc.), there was a need to map alphabetic characters to numbers. The ASCII (American Standard Code for Information Interchange) was developed in the 1960s to map the English alphabetic characters to numbers. ASCII is a coding scheme using 7 or 8 bits to assign numeric values to up to 256 characters, including letters, numerals, punctuation marks, control characters and other symbols. The current ASCII standards map all the printable, non-printable and extended characters on a computer keyboard to numbers (since computers only understand zeros and ones).

The ASCII uses 256 binary digits just like Odu Ifa. This simply means each of the 256 signatures of Odu Ifa can be mapped to every key on the computer keyboard. Let's examine a few chapters of Odu Ifa, with their corresponding binary digits and decimal values, mapped to specific ASCII symbols and characters:

(ASCII Symbol == Decimal Value == Binary Value == Odu Ifa)

Numerals:

0 == 48 == 00110000 == Ogbe-Ọwọnrin

1 == 49 == 00110001 == Ọsa-Ọwọnrin

2 == 50 == 00110010 == Otura-Ọwọnrin

3 == 51 == 00110011 == Ọwọnrin-Meji

4 == 52 == 00110100 == Irẹtẹ-Ọwọnrin

Lowercase characters:

a == 97 == 01100001 == Ọsa-Odi

b == 98 == 01100010 == Otura-Odi

c == 99 == 01100011 == Ọwọnrin-Odi

d == 100 == 01100100 == Irẹtẹ-Odi

e == 101 == 01100101 == Ofun-Odi

Uppercase characters:

A == 65 == 01000001 == Ọsa-Irẹtẹ

B == 66 == 01000010 == Otura-Irẹtẹ

C == 67 == 01000011 == Ọwọnrin-Irẹtẹ

D == 68 == 01000100 == Irẹtẹ-Meji

E == 69 == 01000101 == Ofun-Irẹtẹ

See Appendix B for the charts of all the 256 chapters of Odu Ifa mapped to the 256 ASCII characters on our computer keyboard.

Chapter Eight

Ifa divination system and its convergence with quantum computer systems

Just like the logical operation of the Ikin divinatory instrument converges with the basic logical operation of a digital computer system, the quantum operation of the Ọpẹlẹ divinatory instrument converges with the quantum mechanics of a quantum computer system. Quantum computing is a theoretical design for computers based on quantum mechanics. Unlike classical digital computers, which encode information into binary digits with only two possible values, either a 0 or 1, quantum computers encode information into quantum bits (qubits), which can take the form of 0, 1 or a superposition of both 0 and 1. Similarly, unlike the Ikin, which uses binary digits in its computation, the Ọpẹlẹ quantum chain uses quantum bits, which can take the form of 0, 1 or a superposition of both 0 and 1.

It is my goal, in this chapter, to use the structure and operational mechanics of the Ọpẹlẹ divinatory instrument to show the similarities between the Ifa divination system and quantum computer systems.

What is a quantum computer?

A quantum computer is a type of computer that uses quantum mechanics so that it can perform certain kinds of computation more efficiently than a regular digital computer. Quantum computers perform computations using quantum bits or qubits. One qubit can represent not just 0 or 1 as in regular digital computers, but 0 or 1 or both simultaneously—a phenomenon called "superposition." A pair of qubits can represent four quantum states ($2^2 = 4$), which transitions to two classical bits when measured. Three qubits can represent eight quantum states ($2^3 = 8$), which transition to three classical bits when measured. So, N qubits can represent 2^N quantum states, which transition to N classical bits when measured.

Explanation of fundamental concepts associated with quantum computers

Qubit (short for quantum bit): is the basic unit of information in a quantum computer. Qubits are unlike bits in current computers because they can exist in more than one state at the same time. Compared to a classical bit, which can exist in one of two states, the quantum bit can exist in two states and in any superposition of those two states. The fact that the qubit can be in a superposition simply means it can be "on" and "off" or 0 and 1 simultaneously.

Quantum state: is any of the possible states of a physical system that are specified by a particular attribute of the physical system such as charge or spin. In quantum computing, if k is the number of quantum states, then one quantum bit can have $k = 2^1 = 2$ quantum states. Two quantum bits can have $k = 2^2 = 4$ quantum states. Therefore, N quantum bits can have $k = 2^N$ quantum states.

Quantum superposition: is a quantum phenomenon whereby one particle is in two quantum states at the same time. The best way to picture this phenomenon is to think of a particle in two quantum states as a regular coin with two sides: heads and tails. Accordingly, quantum superposition, in qubits, can be explained by spinning a coin on a flat surface. While the coin is still spinning on the flat surface, the coin is actually in two states (heads and tails) at the same time. Until the coin lands on either side, it has to be considered both heads and tails simultaneously. The principle of quantum superposition is what enables quantum computers to perform certain kinds of computation more efficiciently than a regular digital computer.

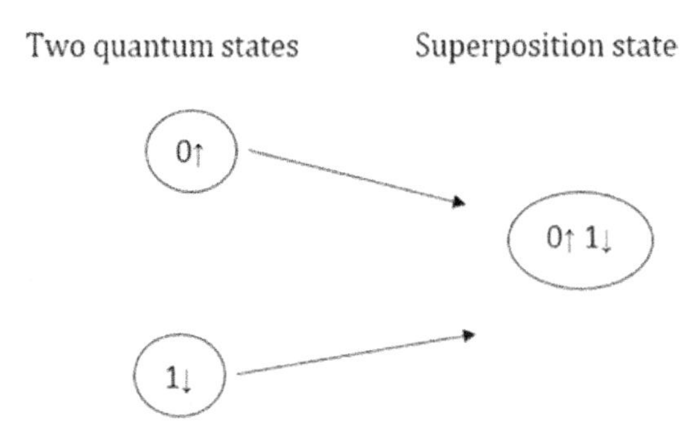

Quantum entanglement: is a phenomenon where two particles in two quantum states are inseparably linked, so that actions performed on one affect the other almost instantaneously. According to Pas (2019):

> Entanglement is nature's way of integrating parts into a whole; individual properties of constituents cease to exist for the benefit of a strongly correlated total system. (par. 12).

To illustrate this phenomenon, let us assume we have two particles (A and B), which are capable of both upward and downward spins. If we represent the upward spin with binary 0 and the downward spin with binary 1, then we can say the two particles are entangled as represented below.

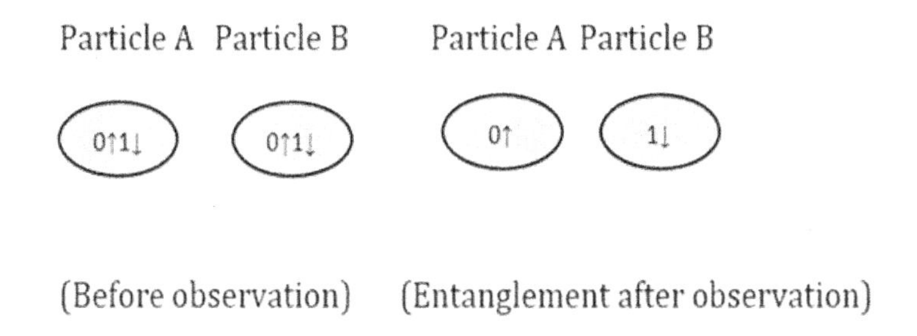

Quantum measurement: in quantum theory, it is presumed that unobserved particle exists in all possible states simultaneously. However, when observed or measured, it exhibits only one state: up or down, 0 or 1, on or off. In other words, observation or measurement effectively destroys superposition, reducing the particle to a single state.

Quantum bits, quantum states, quantum measurement, superposition and entanglement in the Ọpẹlẹ

As previously mentioned in chapter five, in its basic form, the Ọpẹlẹ is a 4x2 quantum chain. It has 8 two-sided quantum tokens (qutokens) arranged in four distinct rows and two parallel columns, and they are all connected by a string. Each qutoken on the left leg of the Ọpẹlẹ chain is structurally entangled with each qutoken on the right. The four qutokens on the left, as those on the right, can give $2^4 = 16$ possible combinations.

$$\text{Left side} = A_i = (i = 1,.., 16)$$
$$\text{Right side} = B_i = (i = 1,.., 16)$$

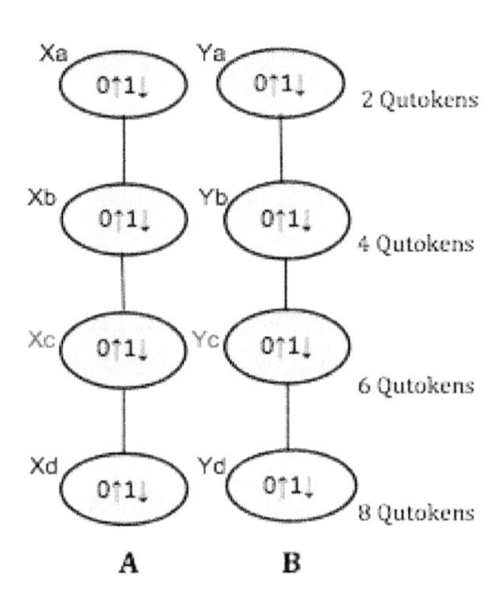

Figure 13. A schematic of the 4x2 Ọpẹlẹ quantum chain in its ground state

Structurally, the Ọpẹlẹ quantum chain appears complex, but its complexity can be made simple by comparing each of its qutokens to a common silver coin. A coin has two superposed sides (heads and tails), and when tossed in the air, a "head" or a "tail" emerges as the outcome, not both and not neither. Now imagine connecting eight different coins, in a 4x2 matrix structure, with a metal string and tossing the string randomly in the air, you get: $2^1 \times 2^1 \times 2^1 \times 2^1 \times 2^1 \times 2^1 \times 2^1 \times 2^1 = 2^8 = 256$ possible outcomes or combinations. The Ọpẹlẹ qutoken, like a regular coin or a qubit, transitions from its superposed state (0 and 1) to a distinct, mutually exclusive state (0 or 1) when observed. In other words, when the Ọpẹlẹ chain is cast on the mat and observed, each of its qutokens transitions from its superposed state (0 and 1) to a distinct state (0 or 1) just as we have it in the conventional digital computer. As such, each Ọpẹlẹ qutoken can be thought of as a quantum bit (qubit) in a quantum computer. And since there are 8 qutokens in the Ọpẹlẹ chain, the Ọpẹlẹ chain can represent $2^8 = 256$ quantum states.

The Ọpẹlẹ quantum chain, just like the quantum computer, operates based on the quantum principle of superposition—that is, unlike a classical bit that can only take one state (0 or 1) at a time and not two states simultaneously, each qutoken in the Ọpẹlẹ chain, like each qubit in a quantum computer, is in a superposition of two distinct states (0 and 1). It is my presumption that the inner workings of a quantum system is similar to the inner workings of the human mind. The human mind assigns varying weights to our thoughts, which are unobservable, and executes the one with the highest weight; the executed thought is what we observe in reality. This explains why qutokens have two sides: concave and convex.

Essentially, qutokens are designed to simulate human thoughts in that every thought in our minds carries two energies (good and bad) simultaneously, and these two energies are in a state of quantum superposition.

Not only do we see the principle of superposition in the Ọpẹlẹ qutokens, but we also see the principle of entanglement. Albert Einstein described the quantum behavior of entanglement as a "spooky action at a distance." The spookiness can be summarized as follows: if a pair of particles are generated in such a way that their total spin is known to be zero, and one particle is found to have clockwise spin on a certain axis, the spin of the other particle, measured on the same axis, will be found to be counterclockwise due to their entanglement. What the physicists call spooky or entanglement is what we call Ọmọ Odu (minor Odu) in Ifa divination system. Let me reduce the "spookiness" to a simple Ifa language that everyone can understand.

During the divination process, when the Ọpẹlẹ quantum chain is excited and is randomly tossed on the ground, the superposed quantum states of each qutoken, as shown in figure 14, collapses into one state as depicted in figure 15, which is consistent with the quantum rule that states that an unobserved particle exists in all possible states simultaneously but, when observed or measured, exhibits only one state: up or down, 0 or 1, on or off.

Left	Right
Xa(0/1)-----	Ya(0/1)
Xb(0/1)-----	Yb(0/1)
Xc(0/1)-----	Yc (0/1)
Xd(0/1)-----	Yd(0/1)

Figure 14. A schematic of the standard 4X2 Ọpẹlẹ quantum chain in its ground state, before it is tossed

So, if it happens that, after the Ọpẹlẹ chain is cast and observed, the qutokens collapse in such a way that the four qutokens on the Ọpẹlẹ's left leg are complementary opposites of those on the right leg, as depicted in figure 15, then we get what the physicists call "QUANTUM ENTANGLEMENT," which we call Ọmọ Odu.

Left	Right
Xa(1)	Ya(0)
Xb(1)	Yb(0)
Xc(1)	Yc(0)
Xd(1)	Yd(0)

Figure 15. A schematic of Odu "Ogbe-Ọyẹku" (a minor Odu)

Essentially, entanglement in quantum systems converges with Ọpẹlẹ's way of integrating eight qutokens into a whole system, whereby individual properties of the constituent qutokens cease to exist for the benefit of a strongly correlated total system: the generation of random Odu Ifa patterns or signatures. Therefore, just as the principle of quantum superposition and entanglement enable quantum computers to perform certain kinds of computation exponentially faster than a regular digital computer, the same principles enable the Ọpẹlẹ quantum chain to process information faster than the Ikin. Table 6 further shows the similarities between the operational structure of the Ọpẹlẹ quantum chain and a quantum computer system.

The Ọpẹlẹ quantum chain	Quantum computer
1. An Ọpẹlẹ quantum token (qutoken) is an observable with two inseparable sides: a concave side and a convex side.	A quantum computer bit (qubit) is also an observable with two inseparable sides: 0 and 1.
2. The two inseparable sides of a qutoken are in a state of quantum superposition.	The two inseparable sides of a qubit are also in a state of quantum superposition.
3. The qutokens are not generally independent of one another. They are arranged in a 4x2 matrix structure in which each qutoken on the left side of the Ọpẹlẹ chain can be entangled with its pair on the right side.	The qubits also are not generally independent of one another; they can get entangled with one another.
4. The Ọpẹlẹ quantum chain operates based on quantum superposition and entanglement.	Quantum computers also operate based on quantum superposition and entanglement.
5. The Ọpẹlẹ quantum chain computes through the use of exponentiation (i.e. 2^n), so as the number of quantum tokens increases, the number of quantum possibilities grows exponentially.	Quantum computers also compute through the use of exponentiation, so as the number of quantum bits (n) increases, the number of quantum states (s) grows exponentially ($s=2^n$).

Table 6. Showing the similarities between the Ọpẹlẹ quantum chain (quchain) and a quantum computer system

Chapter Nine

Decision-making process and Ifa divination system

A person wakes up daily having multiple thoughts on their mind. The mind, they say, is a stream of thoughts. Some people call this stream of thoughts "a range of possibilities" while others call it "a non-linear spectrum of potentialities." Interestingly, a person can only choose one thought out of the multiple possibilities on their mind. Their mind, relying on their ego, emotion, past experiences, introspective intuition, heuristics and available information, comes to the person's rescue by narrowing the plural thoughts down to a manageable number while nature handles the rest, further narrowing the result down to a preferential option. Presented with one preferential option, the person is confused as ever before. In an attempt to overcome the confusion and choose optimally, they seek information through the Ifa divination system, making it easier for them to make a choice.

First and foremost, a person must be free to make a choice. Free choice is the power or ability of humans to make choices free of constraints. The concept of free choice and its existence have long been debated by scholars over the ages. I shall not add to this long debate in this chapter; rather, I shall shed some light on the differences between decision making and choice and the role that the Ifa divination system plays in the probabilistic modeling of the human decision-making process.

Decision making is a process of weighing the merits and demerits of multiple options and narrowing down the options to one. In the most general terms, the decision-making process takes time. During this process, the brain undergoes a transition from possible to actual or from plurality to unity. To illustrate, let's use a restaurant menu as an example. A menu provides information about the food items available at the restaurant along with prices. Equipped with the menu, the customer can begin the decision-making process as to what food item to have for dinner. The customer's decision is not made in a void. It is mostly influenced by a myriad of factors, both internal and external, such as taste, price, health concerns, emotion, past experiences, culture, available information, etc. If the customer finally narrows the food options to having a bowl of chicken salad for dinner and actually orders it, then the customer's dining experience will suddenly transition from decision to choice. So, while decision-making connects to the place of desired intention, judging of options and the mental elimination of options, choice connects to the place of actual selection of an option, execution of desired intention and production of outcomes. In other words, decision-making can be described as the conscious deliberation between options with unclear outcomes, whereas choice is closer to real actions and clear outcomes.

Every preferred option, hidden or revealed, is a superposition of binary outcomes: positive (ire or 0) and negative (ibi or 1). However, when a preferred option is actually acted upon and chosen among the available alternatives, its superposed binary outcomes will suddenly transition to a discrete state where the expected outcome is either positive (ire) or negative (ibi) and not both at the same time. For example, you are a veteran investor who invests only in pharmaceutical stocks. If your investment preference is in the shares of a pharmaceutical company whose product is still in development without FDA approval, there are only two foreseeable outcomes in your investment future—these investment outcomes are in a state of superposition (positive and negative) until you actually execute your investment preference. Now, if you go ahead and execute your investment preference by actually buying the shares of the pharmaceutical company, then either the company's drug will pass the FDA approval or it will not. If the drug passes the FDA approval, its share price might quadruple, and you might end up making a lot of money—a desirable outcome. However, if the drug does not pass the FDA approval, its share price might drop precipitously, and you might lose your initial investment—an undesirable outcome. Note that the moment you exercise your choice and buy the shares of the pharmaceutical company, your expected investment outcomes will transition from the superposed "and" state to a discrete "or" state.

Humans, in general, prefer a positive outcome to a negative outcome. Unfortunately, we do not always have adequate information about the choices that we make, making it, in most cases, difficult for us to predict the outcomes of our choices (positive or negative). Accordingly, the expected outcomes of our choices can best be understood in terms of probability theory. In probability theory, the outcome of every choice that we make has two possible states that are both collectively exhaustive and mutually exclusive. They are collectively exhaustive because at least one of the two possible states must emerge; they are mutually exclusive because only one state is possible at a given time and not both.

For instance, if variable A is used to denote the outcome of an Ọpẹlẹ token toss, since an Ọpẹlẹ token, like a regular coin, has two distinct sides (concave and convex), the outcome of the toss must be either concave or convex and not both. Consequently, the probability of it being either concave or convex and not both is 1 because the probability distribution of A would take the value 0.5 for A = concave and 0.5 for A = convex—that is, P(Aconcave) = 0.5; P(Aconvex) = 0.5 and P(Aconcave or Aconvex) = P(Aconcave) + P(Aconvex) = 0.5+0.5 = 1. Conversely, the probability of the outcome being both concave and convex is 0; that is, P(Aconcave and Aconvex) = 0 since only one side can appear at a given time and not both. I must mention that in a real life event that involves choosing one option among the available alternatives, the actual probability distribution of choosing an option with a positive outcome would start around 0.5 or 50% as in the case of the random Ọpẹlẹ token tossing above, but over time, with the accrual of information, the actual probability distribution would gradually approach 1 or 100%.

In principle, with sufficient computational power and time to mine, evaluate and process information about available options, the outcome of every choice may be predicted with a high degree of certainty. In his theory of bounded rationality, the Nobel Laureate Herbert Simon underscores the importance of information to decision-making process. He argues that a rational agent's ability to make optimized decisions is constrained by the information they have, the cognitive limitations of their computational intelligence, and the finite amount of time they have to evaluate and process information. Clearly, information is vital to our decision-making process. This explains why we have developed different ways of encoding large volumes of information outside our bodies. For example, we encode information in books, audio recordings, videos, computer-readable media, and cyber cloud.

Traditionally, the Yoruba people of West Africa organize, process and retrieve information with the aid of the Ifa divination system. Today, the Ifa divination system is adapted, by many people around the world, to optimize their expected outcomes and to improve their decision-making process. The question now is: how does the Ifa divination system improve our decision-making process?

Before I delve into the explanation of how the Ifa divination system improves our decisions, I should mention that decision making is primarily concerned with the constant weighing of options in the face of a profoundly complex and uncertain world. In this complex and uncertain world, our conventional conception of the human decision-making process as strictly logical must be re-appraised. Although decision outcomes can only be perceived from a logical perspective, the decision-making process appears to be totally probabilistic. I think, therefore, our decision-making process can best be modeled in terms of probability theory because the process is more probabilistic than logical.

There is an underlying practical relevance of probability theory in the operational mechanics of the Ifa divination system; that is, the Ifa divination system models the probabilistic nature of human decision making by introducing a probability distribution defined by its divinatory instruments: the Ọpẹlẹ quantum chain and the Ikin. Essentially, the Ifa divination system employs probability, with the aid of its divinatory instruments, to model people's preferential options and make recommendations about the best possible choice outcome.

Fundamentally, the Ọpẹlẹ quantum chain is designed to capture the computational mechanics of the human mind during its decision-making process. In fact, all the eight qutokens that constitute the Ọpẹlẹ quantum chain are meant to imitate the stream of thoughts running through our minds at any given time. Remember, the human mind is a stream of thoughts and every thought is a superposition of two possible outcomes. When a thought is executed, it quickly transitions from a state of possibility with unclear outcomes to a state of reality with a clear outcome that can be either positive or negative not both and not neither. Similarly, when the Ọpẹlẹ chain is held and gently swung back and forth in the air, each of the two-sided qutokens that constitute the Ọpẹlẹ chain is a superposition of binary outcomes that can be either concave or convex. However, as soon as the Ọpẹlẹ chain is tossed on the ground, each qutoken lies either face up (concave) or face down (convex). And all eight tokens are capable of generating $2 \times 2 \times 2 \times 2 \times 2 \times 2 \times 2 \times 2 = 2^8 = 256$ possible outcomes or patterns. As such, based on the generated pattern, which can be symmetric or asymmetric, the diviner infers back to the corresponding Odu

Ifa in the Odu Ifa knowledge base and retrieves pertinent messages and prescriptions that are needed by the client for their decision making. The client's inquiry is almost always centered on information gathering about a desirable option, hidden or revealed, and its two mutually exclusive expected outcomes.

The Ikin, although operationally more cumbersome than the Ọpẹlẹ quantum chain, is designed for the same purpose, which is the use of probability of numbers to model the complexity of the human thought process. Essentially, the 16 Ikin sacred palm nuts are designed to imitate our stream of thoughts while we make decisions. In fact, the underlying process of manipulating the 16 sacred palm nuts between the left and the right hands share a similarity with the human mind in the process of deciding and choosing of options—that is, in the left hand is the simulation of the mind with its hypothetical 16 range of options, whereas, in the right hand is the outcome of the chosen option that can be either odd (1 or negative) or even (0 or positive) not both and not neither. So, based on the emergent outcome, as in the Ọpẹlẹ-based divination, the diviner will infer back to the Odu Ifa database, retrieve pertinent messages to the client's situation and make prescriptions that are needed by the client.

Lastly, while the lack of adequate information about our choices undoubtedly leads us to describe decision-making as probabilistic, information is not the only factor that regulates human decisions. Empirical research increasingly shows that other latent factors such as emotion, mood, taste, personal loyalty, culture, and a sense of fairness can also regulate human decisions. Consequently, the Ifa divination process goes beyond probability modeling through the manipulation of random binary numbers. It entails the retrieval, from the Odu Ifa knowledge base, of messages that are relevant to the client's situation, the interpretation of these messages for the client and the prescription of certain ethical conducts such as suuru (patience), ẹbọ ruru (sacrifice), ọwọ (respect) and iwapẹlẹ (humility or gentle character), all of which would positively regulate the latent factors that go into the client's decision-making process and consequently optimize the client's choice outcomes.

Chapter Ten

The practical application of Ifa divination system

When I first became seriously interested in Ifa and its divination system, I wanted to learn about the practical applications of the Ifa divination system. Unfortunately, most of the materials I found only talked about the traditional use of the Ifa divination system as a basic divinatory instrument. Having studied the Ifa divination system and the technological information embedded in it for a few years, I realized that the Ifa divination system could be adapted for a wide range of practical applications beyond its traditional use as a basic divinatory instrument. Consequently, I decided to write, in this chapter, what I had wanted to study, but could not find, when I first became seriously interested in Ifa and its divination system.

While the Ifa divination system has practical applications in different areas of human endeavor, the focus of this chapter is on the application of the Ifa divination system in cryptography.

The application of the Ifa divination system in cryptography

The Ọpẹlẹ quantum chain, which is one of the Ifa divinatory instruments, is an excellent pseudo-random number generator; it can generate a sequence that does not have any predictable pattern. The Ọpẹlẹ quchain can generate 256 random binary keys called Odu—each toss of the Ọpẹlẹ quchain produces a random binary key. These 256 binary keys can be combined multiple times ad infinitum to generate pseudo-random numbers. For example, let us assume that after one toss of the Ọpẹlẹ quchain, Odu Ọyẹku-Meji emerges. Odu Ọyẹku-Meji is one of the major chapters of Odu Ifa whose binary key is 11111111. If I give the binary key of Ọyẹku-Meji (11111111) to an intruder free of charge, can the intruder predict accurately, with the Ọyẹku-Meji's binary key, the binary key of the next Ọpẹlẹ cast? No, they cannot. In other words, even if an experienced hacker/intruder can somehow determine or observe the binary key generated by the initial toss of the Ọpẹlẹ quchain, they cannot use the same binary key to predict the binary key of the next toss.

While the binary keys of the 256 chapters of Odu Ifa can be combined multiple times to generate pseudo-random numbers, it is impossible to use the binary key of one chapter of Odu Ifa to predict accurately the binary key of the next. The inability to make an accurate prediction of the binary key of a yet to be generated Odu Ifa, given the binary key of an observed Odu Ifa, is what makes the Ifa divination system a good pseudo-random number generator. Consequently, as a pseudo-random number generator, the Ọpẹlẹ quchain can be adapted for use in cryptography. Let us now explore the Odu Ifa cryptographic technique and the use of Ọpẹlẹ quchain as an encryption device.

Terminology

Encryption: in cryptography, encryption is the process of encoding a message or information in such a way that only authorized parties can access it and those who are not authorized cannot. In other words, encryption denies the intelligible content to a would-be interceptor. In an encryption scheme, the intended message or plaintext is encrypted using an encryption algorithm or a cipher, generating ciphertext that can be read only if decrypted. For technical reasons, an encryption scheme usually uses a pseudo-random encryption number or cipher generated by an algorithm.

Encryption key: is a random sequence of bits generated explicitly for encrypting and decrypting data.

Symmetric key or secret-key encryption: is an encryption process in which the same key is used to encrypt data as it does to decrypt data, and the key must remain secret.

Plain text: an un-encrypted text or message in its original form. It can be a stream of bits, a text file, a bitmap, a stream of digitized voice or a digital video image.

Cipher: an algorithm or mathematical function used for encryption or decryption.

XOR cipher: this is a type of binary additive stream cipher that combines generated binary keystream, bitwise, with plaintext using the exclusive or (XOR) operation. XOR cipher operates according to the principles:

Inputs	Output
$0 \oplus 0 =$	0
$0 \oplus 1 =$	1
$1 \oplus 0 =$	1
$1 \oplus 1 =$	0

Also note that:
$A \oplus A = 0$
$(A \oplus B) \oplus B = A$, where $\oplus$ is the mathematical notation for the XOR operation.
Ciphertext: the scrambled or encoded text of an encrypted message; it is the result or output of an encryption process and the input of a decryption process.

The math

Key Size	Formula	Possible key combinations
1-bit	2^1	2
2-bit	2^2	4
4-bit	2^4	16
8-bit	2^8	256
16-bit	2^{16}	65536
32-bit	2^{32}	4.2×10^9

The implementation

The implementation of the Ọpẹlẹ quchain for encryption and decryption can be divided into four main steps:

1. The creation of the structure of key and input data.
2. The pseudo-random key generation.
3. The creation of the Odubetical ASCII table.
4. The development of the Ọpẹlẹ quchain algorithm.

1. The creation of the structure of key and input data

The Ọpẹlẹ quchain encryption scheme is implemented as a symmetric key or secret-key encryption for encrypting texts that can be decrypted with the original encryption key. Under the Ọpẹlẹ quchain encryption scheme, both the input message (plaintext) and the encryption key are structured as a set of byte arrays. Each byte array, as shown below, comprises a 4x2 unit cell of bits. In other words, each byte array is essentially a 4x2 Ọpẹlẹ quchain.

Plaintext

Left leg (L) Right leg (R)

P4	P0
P5	P1
P6	P2
P7	P3

....

Pn_4	Pn_0
Pn_5	Pn_1
Pn_6	Pn2
Pn_7	Pn_3

Key

Left leg (L) Right leg (R)

K4	K0
K5	K1
K6	K2
K7	K3

....

Kn_4	Kn_0
Kn_5	Kn_1
Kn_6	Kn_2
Kn_7	Kn_3

Figure 16. The structure of the key and input data

2. The pseudo-random key generation

The Ọpẹlẹ quchain can be used as a pseudo-random number generator through the process of modulo 2 recursion. The Ọpẹlẹ quchain is cast to generate eight random bits; the last two bits are added together; the result is divided by two; the remainder of the division is placed in the first position and other bits are shifted to the right, with the last bit discarded. This 8-bit shift recursive process will produce 255 random keys before the cycle repeats, but the period of the cycle and the number of keys generated increase with more bits ($2^n - 1$). In other words, if the 4x2 Ọpẹlẹ quchain is modified into an 8x2 Ọpẹlẹ quchain, the number of keys generated will increase to $2^{16} - 1 = 65,535$. In cryptography, the larger the key size, the harder it is for the encrypted message to be deciphered and the more secured the encrypted message is. So, structurally, if the Ọpẹlẹ quchain is to be used as a fairly secured cryptographic device, its traditional 4x2 matrix structure must be modified, at a minimum, to an 8x2 matrix structure—an 8x2 Ọpẹlẹ Quchain has $2^{16} = 65,536$ possible key combinations.

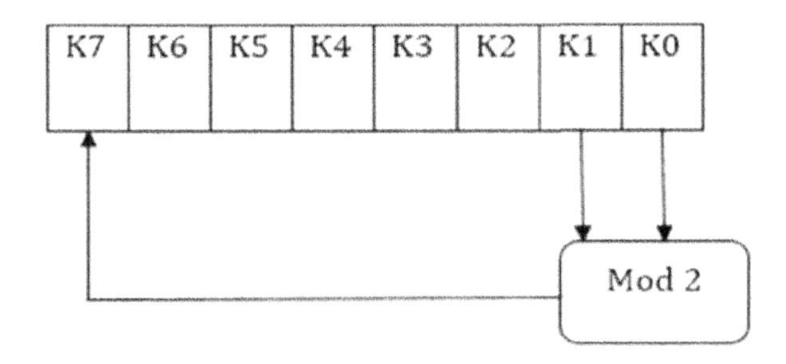

Figure 17. A schematic of the process of mod 2 recursion

3. The creation of the Odubetical ASCII table

The Odubetical ASCII table is created by mapping each of the 256 chapters of Odu Ifa, with its corresponding 8-bit binary code, to a specific ASCII character or symbol. It should be remembered that each of the 256 ASCII characters and symbols has its own corresponding 8-bit binary code just like each chapter of Odu Ifa. So, in the Odubetical ASCII table, each Odu Ifa is mapped to an ASCII character or symbol that shares its 8-bit binary code. Let us look at a few examples. The lower-case letter "a" on your computer keyboard and the minor Odu “Ọsa-Odi” both share the same 8-bit binary code, “01100001.” So, the two are mapped to each other in the Odubetical table as follows: a = Ọsa-Odi = 01100001. Similarly, the capital letter “B” on your keyboard and the minor Odu “Otura-Irẹtẹ” both share the same 8-bit binary code, “01000010.” They too are mapped to each other as follows: B = Otura-Irẹtẹ = 01000010—this continues until all the 256 chapters of Odu Ifa are completely mapped to their corresponding ASCII characters and symbols (see appendix B).

4. The development of the Ọpẹlẹ quchain algorithm

The Ọpẹlẹ quchain algorithm is implemented as an XOR operation. In this operation, the input message is encrypted by dividing the 8-bit ASCII code of each character of the input message into two blocks or legs and applying the bitwise XOR operator on both legs of the input message using a key generated by the Ọpẹlẹ quchain. Conversely, to decrypt the encrypted message (i.e. cipher text), repeating the XOR operation with the key will remove the cipher. So, if the input message to be sent to the receiver is denoted by $M_{(L,R)}$, the encryption key by $E_{k(L,R)}$ and the cipher text by $C_{(L,R)}$ then the encryption operation can be represented as follows:

$$M_{(L,R)} \oplus E_{k(L,R)} = C_{(L,R)}$$

and conversely, for decryption:

$$C_{(L,R)} \oplus E_{k(L,R)} = M_{(L,R)}$$

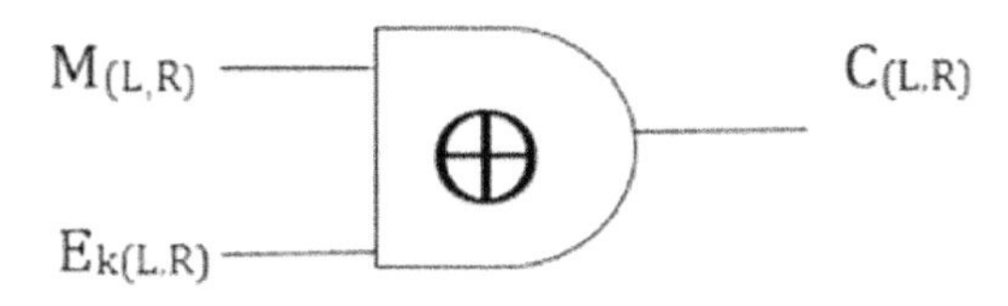

Figure 18. Encryption operation

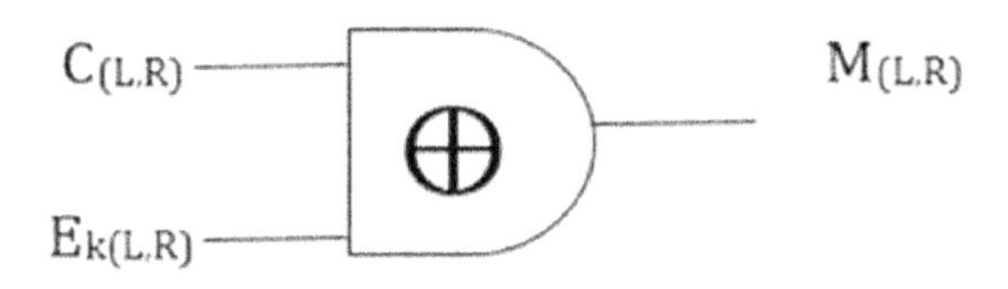

Figure 19. Decryption operation

For example, let us assume that a sender A wants to send the word "go" as an encrypted message to a receiver B. The word "go" in two sets of 8-bit (2 bytes) ASCII can be represented as follows: g = 01100111 = Ọkanran-Odi and o = 01101111 = Ọyẹku-Odi. To encrypt and send this message (M), sender A has to use a modified 8x2 Ọpẹlẹ quchain to randomly generate an encryption key (E_k). Now, let's also assume that the randomly generated encryption key is a repeating binary key of Ọyẹku-Meji (11111111 11111111)—note: Ọyẹku-Meji's binary key is 11111111. The structure of the repeating key and the input data are depicted as follows:

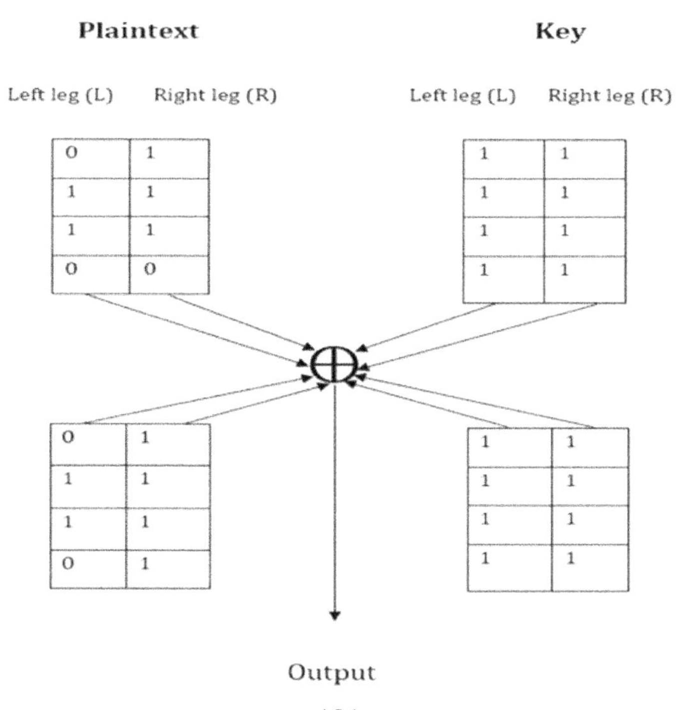

So, for encryption:

the input message, "go" = 0110-0111 0110-1111 = Ọkanran-Odi Ọyẹku-Odi

XOR

Encryption key = 1111-1111 1111-1111 = Ọyẹku-Meji Ọyẹku-Meji
Cipher (Output) = 1001-1000 1001-0000 = Ogunda-Iwori Ogbe-Iwori

And conversely, for decryption:

Cipher (Input) = 1001-1000 1001-0000 = Ogunda-Iwori Ogbe-Iwori

XOR

Encryption key = 11111111 11111111 = Ọyẹku-Meji Ọyẹku-Meji
Message (Output) = 0110-0111 0110-1111 = "go"

5. The implementation of the Ọpẹlẹ quantum chain algorithm

The Ọpẹlẹ quantum chain algorithm is very easy to implement; it can be implemented using any of the popular programming languages. However, for higher encryption security, the algorithm structure can be modified to incorporate more sophisticated encryption operations, but those operations are beyond the scope of this book. Appendix A shows the implementation of the Ọpẹlẹ quchain algorithm with a python programming language.

Epilogue

I strongly believe that the ability of humans to invent abstract concepts and subscribe to them, in large numbers, is the principal driver of human progress and civilization because subscribing to a common abstraction, in large numbers, creates mutual trust among the people, facilitates social cooperation, ameliorates social conflict and promotes nation building. As such, for a group of people to progress, in this world, and build a sustainable civilization, they must be able to subscribe to a common abstraction or story: myths, deities, spiritual philosophy and other “isms.” Unfortunately, when I look at Africa, specifically Yorubaland, I see a society where the people neither promote their traditional abstractions nor invent new ones. They mostly subscribe to different foreign abstractions. By the way, foreign abstractions are not necessarily bad except that they are often divisive and not germane to the local realities in Africa.

The question now is, if indeed subscribing to a common abstraction in large numbers creates mutual trust among the people, facilitates social cooperation, ameliorates social conflict and promotes nation building, what common or unifying abstraction should Africans embrace in order to build a progressive civilization? I cannot speak for other African nations, but I can speak for the Yorubaland. I think Yorubaland should accommodate different abstractions or systems, but the unifying one must be Ifa.

Why Ifa?

1. Ifa is the Yoruba knowledge base or the literary corpus of Yoruba mythology, epistemology, metaphysics, philosophy (moral, spiritual and natural philosophies), cosmology, and natural science. As such, without Ifa, the Yoruba, as a collective, would be empty.
2. It is not enough to have a unifying abstraction or a common story that appeals to the populace, the abstraction must be malleable

or adaptable to the present reality because human reality is dynamic and not static. Accordingly, Ifa should be nationally embraced because we find in the Ifa divination system some elements of mathematical, philosophical and technological knowledge that are relevant to the current information technology world.

3. In terms of information processing, the Ifa divination system converges not only with digital computers but also with quantum computers. In addition, the Ifa divination system has relevant applications in cryptography and quantum physics.

All in all, Ifa is qualified to be a unifying system in the Yorubaland because not only is it an indigenous system, its divination system, if properly studied and promoted, has some elements of mathematical, philosophical and technological knowledge that are useful in today's information technology world.

Appendix A

Implementation of the Ọpẹlẹ quchain algorithm with a python programming language

```
#!/usr/bin/env python3

'''Odu Ifa Encryption
  oducryption.py
```

This python module implements the XOR encryption by using the 256 Odu Ifa signatures from: Eji-Ogbe to Ọyẹku-Meji

Below are some of the mappings from Odu Ifa to Binary, Decimal and Hexadecimal.

```
Binary     Decimal  Hexadecimal  Odu Ifa
--------   -------  -----------  --------
00000000      0       \x00       Eji-Ogbe
00000001      1       \x01       Ọsa-Ogbe
00000010      2       \x02       Otura-Ogbe
00000011      3       \x03       Ọwọnrin-Ogbe
00000100      4       \x04       Irẹtẹ-Ogbe
00000101      5       \x05       Ofun-Ogbe
00000110      6       \x06       Odi-Ogbe
00000111      7       \x07       Ọkanran-Ogbe
00001000      8       \x08       Ogunda-Ogbe
00001001      9       \t         Iwori-Ogbe
00001010     10       \n         Ọsẹ-Ogbe
00001011     11       \x0b       Oturupọn-Ogbe
00001100     12       \x0c       Irosun-Ogbe
00001101     13       \r         Ika-Ogbe
00001110     14       \x0e       Ọbara-Ogbe
00001111     15       \x0f       Ọyẹku-Ogbe

  It requires Python3 to run
'''


import random
import string
import sys

def generate_odu_characters():
   '''Function to generate all the 256 ascii characters that
map to Odu Ifa
   '''
   return [chr(i) for i in range(256)]


def cast_Ọpẹlẹ(number_of_times):
```

```
    '''Function to simulate the casting of the Ọpẹlẹ chain.

    The function takes one parameter: number of times to
throw the Ọpẹlẹ chain
    This generate random characters from the 256 Odu
    '''

    # Generate random Odu
    secure_random = random.SystemRandom()
    odu_chars = generate_odu_characters()
    return ''.join([secure_random.choice(odu_chars) for _ in
range(number_of_times)])


def odu_cipher (message, secret_key):
    '''Function to either encrypt or decrypt a message with
the appropriate key.

    The function takes two parameters:
    (1) message to encrypt or decrypt
    (2) secret key generated by the cast_Ọpẹlẹ function

    The function returns either an encrypted text or
decrypted text depending on
    the message. It uses XOR encryption algorithm. This
encryption is unbreakable
    if key is larger than message.
    '''

    # Ensure that the length of the key is the same as that of
the  message (pad it up with '0')
    encryption_key = secret_key.ljust(len(message),'0')

    # Encrypt or Decrypt as appropriate with the given secret
key using XOR
    result = [chr (ord (a) ^ ord (b) ) for a, b in zip (message,
encryption_key)]
    return ''.join(result)
```

```
if __name__ == '__main__':
    print()
    message = input('Please enter message: ')
    print()
    binary_message =  ' '.join(['{0:08b}'.format(ord(m), 'b')
for m in message])
    print('Your message in binary format is: ',
binary_message)
    print()
    key_question = input('Do you want the system to
generate random key for you? Y/N: ')
    print()
    key = ''
    if key_question.upper() == 'Y':
      key = cast_Ọpẹlẹ(10)
    else:
      key = input('Please enter your secret key: ')

    if len(key.strip()) == 0:
      print('No secret key provided!')
      print('Exiting...')
      sys.exit(1)

    print('Secret key is: ' + repr(key))
    binary_key = ' '.join(['{0:08b}'.format(ord(x), 'b') for x
in key])
    print()
    print('Secret key in binary format: ', binary_key)
    print()
    encrypted_message = odu_cipher(message, key)
    print('Encrypted message is: ' +
repr(encrypted_message))
    print()
    binary_encrypted_message =  '
'.join(['{0:08b}'.format(ord(e), 'b') for e in
encrypted_message])
    print('Encrypted message in binary format is: ',
binary_encrypted_message)
```

```
    print()
    print()
    print('Decrypting the message at the other end with the
secret key...')
    print()
    decrypted_message = odu_cipher(encrypted_message,
key)
    print('Decrypted message is: ', decrypted_message)
    print()
```

```
MacBook-Pro:misc$ ./oducryption.py

Please enter message: Attack Ilorin at dawn

Your message in binary format is:  01000001
01110100 01110100 01100001 01100011 01101011
00100000 01001001 01101100 01101111 01110010
01101001 01101110 00100000 01100001 01110100
00100000 01100100 01100001 01110111 01101110

Do you want the system to generate random key
for you? Y/N: Y

Secret key is: 'Á³®1w/\tzö»'

Secret key in binary format:  11000001 10110011
10101110 00110001 01110111 00101111 00001001
01111010 11110110 10111011

Encrypted message is:
'\x80ÇÚP\x14D)3\x9aÔBY^\x10QD\x10TQG^'

Encrypted message in binary format is:  10000000
11000111 11011010 01010000 00010100 01000100
00101001 00110011 10011010 11010100 01000010
01011001 01011110 00010000 01010001 01000100
00010000 01010100 01010001 01000111 01011110


Decrypting the message at the other end with the
secret key...
```

```
Decrypted message is:  Attack Ilorin at dawn


==================================================
==================================================
==================================================
==================================================
============================================


MacBook-Pro:misc$ ./oducryption.py

Please enter message: Tell Ogendengbe to get the
generals ready

Your message in binary format is:  01010100
01100101 01101100 01101100 00100000 01001111
01100111 01100101 01101110 01100100 01100101
01101110 01100111 01100010 01100101 00100000
01110100 01101111 00100000 01100111 01100101
01110100 00100000 01110100 01101000 01100101
00100000 01100111 01100101 01101110 01100101
01110010 01100001 01101100 01110011 00100000
01110010 01100101 01100001 01100100 01111001

Do you want the system to generate random key
for you? Y/N: N

Please enter your secret key: operation gbegude
Secret key is: 'operation gbegude'

Secret key in binary format:  01101111 01110000
01100101 01110010 01100001 01110100 01101001
01101111 01101110 00100000 01100111 01100010
01100101 01100111 01110101 01100100 01100101

Encrypted message is:
';\x15\t\x1eA;\x0e\n\x00D\x02\x0c\x02\x05\x10D\x
11_\x10WUD\x10DXU\x10WU^UBQ\\C\x10BUQTI'

Encrypted message in binary format is:  00111011
00010101 00001001 00011110 01000001 00111011
00001110 00001010 00000000 01000100 00000010
00001100 00000010 00000101 00010000 01000100
00010001 01011111 00010000 01010111 01010101
```

```
01000100 00010000 01000100 01011000 01010101
00010000 01010111 01010101 01011110 01010101
01000010 01010001 01011100 01000011 00010000
01000010 01010101 01010001 01010100 01001001
```

```
Decrypting the message at the other end with the
secret key...

Decrypted message is:  Tell Ogendengbe to get
the generals ready
```

Appendix B

Odubetical chart (Odu-ASCII chart). Binary_Decimal_Hex & ASCII Symbols_Odu Ifa

Binary	Decimal	Hex & ASCII	Odu Ifa
00000000	0	\x00	Eji-Ogbe
00000001	1	\x01	Ọsa-Ogbe
00000010	2	\x02	Otura-Ogbe
00000011	3	\x03	Ọwọnrin-Ogbe
00000100	4	\x04	Irẹtẹ-Ogbe
00000101	5	\x05	Ofun-Ogbe
00000110	6	\x06	Odi-Ogbe
00000111	7	\x07	Ọkanran-Ogbe
00001000	8	\x08	Ogunda-Ogbe

00001001	9	\t	Iwori-Ogbe
00001010	10	\n	Ọsẹ-Ogbe
00001011	11	\x0b	Oturupọn-Ogbe
00001100	12	\x0c	Irosun-Ogbe
00001101	13	\r	Ika-Ogbe
00001110	14	\x0e	Ọbara-Ogbe
00001111	15	\x0f	Ọyẹku-Ogbe
00010000	16	\x10	Ogbe-Ọsa
00010001	17	\x11	Ọsa-Meji
00010010	18	\x12	Otura-Ọsa
00010011	19	\x13	Ọwọnrin-Ọsa
00010100	20	\x14	Irẹtẹ-Ọsa
00010101	21	\x15	Ofun-Ọsa
00010110	22	\x16	Odi-Ọsa
00010111	23	\x17	Ọkanran-Ọsa
00011000	24	\x18	Ogunda-Ọsa
00011001	25	\x19	Iwori-Ọsa
00011010	26	\x1a	Ọsẹ-Ọsa
00011011	27	\x1b	Oturupọn-Ọsa
00011100	28	\x1c	Irosun-Ọsa
00011101	29	\x1d	Ika-Ọsa
00011110	30	\x1e	Ọbara-Ọsa
00011111	31	\x1f	Ọyẹku-Ọsa
00100000	32	space	Ogbe-Otura
00100001	33	!	Ọsa-Otura
00100010	34	"	Otura-Meji
00100011	35	#	Ọwọnrin-Otura

00100100	36	$	Irẹtẹ-Otura
00100101	37	%	Ofun-Otura
00100110	38	&	Odi-Otura
00100111	39	),	Ọkanran-Otura
00101000	40	(	Ogunda-Otura
00101001	41	)	Iwori-Otura
00101010	42	*	Ọsẹ-Otura
00101011	43	=+	Oturupọn-Otura
00101100	44	,	Irosun-Otura
00101101	45	-	Ika-Otura
00101110	46	.	Ọbara-Otura
00101111	47	/	Ọyẹku-Otura
00110000	48	0	Ogbe-Ọwọnrin
00110001	49	1	Ọsa-Ọwọnrin
00110010	50	2	Otura-Ọwọnrin
00110011	51	3	Ọwọnrin-Meji
00110100	52	4	Irẹtẹ-Ọwọnrin
00110101	53	5	Ofun-Ọwọnrin
00110110	54	6	Odi-Ọwọnrin
00110111	55	7	Ọkanran-Ọwọnrin
00111000	56	8	Ogunda-Ọwọnrin
00111001	57	9	Iwori-Ọwọnrin
00111010	58	:	Ọsẹ-Ọwọnrin
00111011	59	;	Oturupọn-Ọwọnrin
00111100	60	<	Irosun-Ọwọnrin
00111101	61	=	Ika-Ọwọnrin
00111110	62	>	Ọbara-Ọwọnrin

00111111	63	?	Ọyẹku-Ọwọnrin
01000000	64	@	Ogbe-Irẹtẹ
01000001	65	A	Ọsa-Irẹtẹ
01000010	66	B	Otura-Irẹtẹ
01000011	67	C	Ọwọnrin-Irẹtẹ
01000100	68	D	Irẹtẹ-Meji
01000101	69	E	Ofun-Irẹtẹ
01000110	70	F	Odi-Irẹtẹ
01000111	71	G	Ọkanran-Irẹtẹ
01001000	72	H	Ogunda-Irẹtẹ
01001001	73	I	Iwori-Irẹtẹ
01001010	74	J	Ọsẹ-Irẹtẹ
01001011	75	K	Oturupọn-Irẹtẹ
01001100	76	L	Irosun-Irẹtẹ
01001101	77	M	Ika-Irẹtẹ
01001110	78	N	Ọbara-Irẹtẹ
01001111	79	O	Ọyẹku-Irẹtẹ
01010000	80	P	Ogbe-Ofun
01010001	81	Q	Ọsa-Ofun
01010010	82	R	Otura-Ofun
01010011	83	S	Ọwọnrin-Ofun
01010100	84	T	Irẹtẹ-Ofun
01010101	85	U	Ofun-Meji
01010110	86	V	Odi-Ofun
01010111	87	W	Ọkanran-Ofun
01011000	88	X	Ogunda-Ofun
01011001	89	Y	Iwori-Ofun

01011010	90	Z	Ọsẹ-Ofun
01011011	91	[	Oturupọn-Ofun
01011100	92	\\	Irosun-Ofun
01011101	93	]	Ika-Ofun
01011110	94	^	Ọbara-Ofun
01011111	95	_	Ọyẹku-Ofun
01100000	96	`	Ogbe-Odi
01100001	97	a	Ọsa-Odi
01100010	98	b	Otura-Odi
01100011	99	c	Ọwọnrin-Odi
01100100	100	d	Irẹtẹ-Odi
01100101	101	e	Ofun-Odi
01100110	102	f	Odi-Meji
01100111	103	g	Ọkanran-Odi
01101000	104	h	Ogunda-Odi
01101001	105	i	Iwori-Odi
01101010	106	j	Ọsẹ-Odi
01101011	107	k	Oturupọn-Odi
01101100	108	l	Irosun-Odi
01101101	109	m	Ika-Odi
01101110	110	n	Ọbara-Odi
01101111	111	o	Ọyẹku-Odi
01110000	112	p	Ogbe-Ọkanran
01110001	113	q	Ọsa-Ọkanran
01110010	114	r	Otura-Ọkanran
01110011	115	s	Ọwọnrin-Ọkanran
01110100	116	t	Irẹtẹ-Ọkanran

<table>
<tr><td>01110101</td><td>117</td><td>u</td><td>Ofun-Ọkanran</td></tr>
<tr><td>01110110</td><td>118</td><td>v</td><td>Odi-Ọkanran</td></tr>
<tr><td>01110111</td><td>119</td><td>w</td><td>Ọkanran-Meji</td></tr>
<tr><td>01111000</td><td>120</td><td>x</td><td>Ogunda-Ọkanran</td></tr>
<tr><td>01111001</td><td>121</td><td>y</td><td>Iwori-Ọkanran</td></tr>
<tr><td>01111010</td><td>122</td><td>z</td><td>Ọsẹ-Ọkanran</td></tr>
<tr><td>01111011</td><td>123</td><td>{</td><td>Oturupọn-Ọkanran</td></tr>
<tr><td>01111100</td><td>124</td><td>|</td><td>Irosun-Ọkanran</td></tr>
<tr><td>01111101</td><td>125</td><td>}</td><td>Ika-Ọkanran</td></tr>
<tr><td>01111110</td><td>126</td><td>~</td><td>Ọbara-Ọkanran</td></tr>
<tr><td>01111111</td><td>127</td><td>\x7f</td><td>Ọyẹku-Ọkanran</td></tr>
<tr><td>10000000</td><td>128</td><td>\x80</td><td>Ogbe-Ogunda</td></tr>
<tr><td>10000001</td><td>129</td><td>\x81</td><td>Ọsa-Ogunda</td></tr>
<tr><td>10000010</td><td>130</td><td>\x82</td><td>Otura-Ogunda</td></tr>
<tr><td>10000011</td><td>131</td><td>\x83</td><td>Ọwọnrin-Ogunda</td></tr>
<tr><td>10000100</td><td>132</td><td>\x84</td><td>Irẹtẹ-Ogunda</td></tr>
<tr><td>10000101</td><td>133</td><td>\x85</td><td>Ofun-Ogunda</td></tr>
<tr><td>10000110</td><td>134</td><td>\x86</td><td>Odi-Ogunda</td></tr>
<tr><td>10000111</td><td>135</td><td>\x87</td><td>Ọkanran-Ogunda</td></tr>
<tr><td>10001000</td><td>136</td><td>\x88</td><td>Ogunda-Meji</td></tr>
<tr><td>10001001</td><td>137</td><td>\x89</td><td>Iwori-Ogunda</td></tr>
<tr><td>10001010</td><td>138</td><td>\x8a</td><td>Ọsẹ-Ogunda</td></tr>
<tr><td>10001011</td><td>139</td><td>\x8b</td><td>Oturupọn-Ogunda</td></tr>
<tr><td>10001100</td><td>140</td><td>\x8c</td><td>Irosun-Ogunda</td></tr>
<tr><td>10001101</td><td>141</td><td>\x8d</td><td>Ika-Ogunda</td></tr>
<tr><td>10001110</td><td>142</td><td>\x8e</td><td>Ọbara-Ogunda</td></tr>
<tr><td>10001111</td><td>143</td><td>\x8f</td><td>Ọyẹku-Ogunda</td></tr>
</table>

10010000	144	\x90	Ogbe-Iwori
10010001	145	\x91	Ọsa-Iwori
10010010	146	\x92	Otura-Iwori
10010011	147	\x93	Ọwọnrin-Iwori
10010100	148	\x94	Irẹtẹ-Iwori
10010101	149	\x95	Ofun-Iwori
10010110	150	\x96	Odi-Iwori
10010111	151	\x97	Ọkanran-Iwori
10011000	152	\x98	Ogunda-Iwori
10011001	153	\x99	Iwori-Meji
10011010	154	\x9a	Ọsẹ-Iwori
10011011	155	\x9b	Oturupọn-Iwori
10011100	156	\x9c	Irosun-Iwori
10011101	157	\x9d	Ika-Iwori
10011110	158	\x9e	Ọbara-Iwori
10011111	159	\x9f	Ọyẹku-Iwori
10100000	160	\xa0	Ogbe-Ọsẹ
10100001	161	¡	Ọsa-Ọsẹ
10100010	162	¢	Otura-Ọsẹ
10100011	163	£	Ọwọnrin-Ọsẹ
10100100	164	¤	Irẹtẹ-Ọsẹ
10100101	165	¥	Ofun-Ọsẹ
10100110	166	¦	Odi-Ọsẹ
10100111	167	§	Ọkanran-Ọsẹ
10101000	168	¨	Ogunda-Ọsẹ
10101001	169	©	Iwori-Ọsẹ
10101010	170	ª	Ọsẹ-Meji

10101011	171	«	Oturupọn-Ọsẹ
10101100	172	¬	Irosun-Ọsẹ
10101101	173	\xad	Ika-Ọsẹ
10101110	174	®	Ọbara-Ọsẹ
10101111	175	¯	Ọyẹku-Ọsẹ
10110000	176	°	Ogbe-Oturupọn
10110001	177	±	Ọsa-Oturupọn
10110010	178	²	Otura-Oturupọn
10110011	179	³	Ọwọnrin-Oturupọn
10110100	180	´	Irẹtẹ-Oturupọn
10110101	181	µ	Ofun-Oturupọn
10110110	182	¶	Odi-Oturupọn
10110111	183	·	Ọkanran-Oturupọn
10111000	184	¸	Ogunda-Oturupọn
10111001	185	¹	Iwori-Oturupọn
10111010	186	º	Ọsẹ-Oturupọn
10111011	187	»	Oturupọn-Meji
10111100	188	¼	Irosun-Oturupọn
10111101	189	½	Ika-Oturupọn
10111110	190	¾	Ọbara-Oturupọn
10111111	191	¿	Ọyẹku-Oturupọn
11000000	192	À	Ogbe-Irosun
11000001	193	Á	Ọsa-Irosun
11000010	194	Â	Otura-Irosun
11000011	195	Ã	Ọwọnrin-Irosun
11000100	196	Ä	Irẹtẹ-Irosun
11000101	197	Å	Ofun-Irosun

11000110	198	Æ	Odi-Irosun
11000111	199	Ç	Ọkanran-Irosun
11001000	200	È	Ogunda-Irosun
11001001	201	É	Iwori-Irosun
11001010	202	Ê	Ọsẹ-Irosun
11001011	203	Ë	Oturupọn-Irosun
11001100	204	Ì	Irosun-Meji
11001101	205	Í	Ika-Irosun
11001110	206	Î	Ọbara-Irosun
11001111	207	Ï	Ọyẹku-Irosun
11010000	208	Ð	Ogbe-Ika
11010001	209	Ñ	Ọsa-Ika
11010010	210	Ò	Otura-Ika
11010011	211	Ó	Ọwọnrin-Ika
11010100	212	Ô	Irẹtẹ-Ika
11010101	213	Õ	Ofun-Ika
11010110	214	Ö	Odi-Ika
11010111	215	×	Ọkanran-Ika
11011000	216	Ø	Ogunda-Ika
11011001	217	Ù	Iwori-Ika
11011010	218	Ú	Ọsẹ-Ika
11011011	219	Û	Oturupọn-Ika
11011100	220	Ü	Irosun-Ika
11011101	221	Ý	Ika-Meji
11011110	222	Þ	Ọbara-Ika
11011111	223	ß	Ọyẹku-Ika
11100000	224	à	Ogbe-Ọbara

11100001	225	á	Ọsa-Ọbara
11100010	226	â	Otura-Ọbara
11100011	227	ã	Ọwọnrin-Ọbara
11100100	228	ä	Irẹtẹ-Ọbara
11100101	229	å	Ofun-Ọbara
11100110	230	æ	Odi-Ọbara
11100111	231	ç	Ọkanran-Ọbara
11101000	232	è	Ogunda-Ọbara
11101001	233	é	Iwori-Ọbara
11101010	234	ê	Ọsẹ-Ọbara
11101011	235	ë	Oturupọn-Ọbara
11101100	236	ì	Irosun-Ọbara
11101101	237	í	Ika-Ọbara
11101110	238	î	Ọbara-Meji
11101111	239	ï	Ọyẹku-Ọyẹku
11110000	240	ð	Ogbe-Ọyẹku
11110001	241	ñ	Ọsa-Ọyẹku
11110010	242	ò	Otura-Ọyẹku
11110011	243	ó	Ọwọnrin-Ọyẹku
11110100	244	ô	Irẹtẹ-Ọyẹku
11110101	245	õ	Ofun-Ọyẹku
11110110	246	ö	Odi-Ọyẹku
11110111	247	÷	Ọkanran-Ọyẹku
11111000	248	ø	Ogunda-Ọyẹku
11111001	249	ù	Iwori-Ọyẹku
11111010	250	ú	Ọsẹ-Ọyẹku
11111011	251	û	Oturupọn-Ọyẹku

11111100	252	ü	Irosun-Ọyẹku
11111101	253	ý	Ika-Ọyẹku
11111110	254	þ	Ọbara-Ọyẹku
11111111	255	ÿ	Ọyẹku-Meji

Glossary of terms

Orịṣa – The word "Orịṣa" is a portmanteau of two Yoruba words: Ori and ṣa. "Ori" is the metaphysical head, the initial condition or the internal causality that drives human destiny; whereas, "ṣa" simply means pick or choose. As such, the Orịṣa are those who have been chosen to fulfill a specific purpose; they are visible manifestations of the divine essence.

There are 401 Orịṣa in Yorubaland: Ṣango, Eṣu, Ogun, Ọya, Ọṣun, just to name a few. Each Orịṣa is associated with specific forces in nature. For instance, Ṣango is associated with fire, lightning and thunder. Ogun is associated with iron and metal. Ọya is associated with wind and storm.

Many people refer to the Orịṣa as Yoruba gods and deities.

Oritamẹta – A term meaning "the crossroad or T-junction." Oritamẹta has three paths: the familiar path and two unfamiliar paths. The two unfamiliar paths are mutually exclusive—that is, the path of ire (success) or the path of ibi (failure). Metaphysically, Oritamẹta is the crossroad where tough decisions are made. This explains why, in the absence of perfect information, humans experience confusion at the crossroad. Accordingly, to allay the confusion, the traditional Yoruba people engage in information gathering through periodic divination.

Ori – A term meaning "head." Metaphysically, Ori is the immaterial head and the determinant of the outcome of human events. While most people associate Ori with destiny, Ori is certainly not the only factor that controls the outcome of human actions. Human actions can be traced back to specific internal and external causalities. Ori, I believe, is the internal causality or the initial condition.

If humans were digital computers, Ori would be the hardware, and periodic divination would be the software. In digital computers, the hardware is fixed, but the software is "soft" and flexible. While the hardware is what makes the computer powerful, it is the ability to run different software programs that makes it flexible. Similarly, while our Ori is what makes us strong and powerful, the ability to offer sacrifices (ẹbọ ruru) and engage in information gathering through periodic divination is what guides our Ori, and vicariously us, to the path of ire (success). This explains why the Yoruba traditionalists often say; b'onii ti ri ọla o ri bẹẹ, lo n mu Babalawo d'ifa ọrọọrun, which may be equated to the English saying "the dynamic nature of reality is what necessitates periodic divination."

Eṣu – Arguably the most powerful Yoruba Oriṣa, who is universally recognized and appealed to by all Yoruba regardless of their affiliation to other cults. Eṣu is the divine communicator and mediator between the Oriṣa and humans, the symbol of harmony, and the metaphysical guardian of Oritamẹta.

As the mediator between the Oriṣa and men, Eṣu plays a role in the cults of other Oriṣa, especially that of Ṣango, the powerful Oriṣa of thunder. Eṣu also has a close relationship with Ọrunmila, the Oriṣa of wisdom and divination. The relationship between Eṣu and Ọrunmila is grounded in many myths. One myth states that it was Eṣu who taught Ọrunmila the art of divination. In return, Eṣu asked Ọrunmila for a portion of every prescribed sacrificial offering. Eṣu, therefore, has a vested interest in the process of Ifa divination. This is why most Babalawo advise their clients to offer a sacrifice to Eṣu.

As the symbol of harmony, Eṣu often tries to achieve harmony between disharmonious elements. And as the metaphysical guardian of the crossroad, Eṣu can keep peace in the marketplace and watch over the passageways and transition points in our lives. This explains why Oriṣa adherents offer sacrifices to Eṣu at the crossroads or at the passageways by the marketplace.

Lastly, Eṣu is many things, but he is neither the existential enemy of Olodumare (the Yoruba Godhead) nor is he the bringer of evil on Earth. Eṣu is certainly not equivalent to Satan or the devil as implied by Bishop Ajayi Crowther in his Yoruba translation of the King James Bible.

Tayewo and Kẹyinde – The first born of a set of twins is called Tayewo; meaning, the "first to taste the world" while the second born is called Kẹyinde; meaning, "one who arrives last." In Yorubaland, twins are highly venerated, for they are believed to be corporeal manifestations of the metaphysical concept of tibi tire. Accordingly, twins are elevated to the status of the Orișa in the Yoruba society.

Tibi tire – The Yoruba metaphysical concept that portrays reality as a dynamic union of complementary opposites: good and evil, fortune and misfortune, even and odd, peace and chaos, and so on. In English, it is called binary complementarity or complementary dualism.

Neils Bohr popularized the concept of complementarity in the scientific community when he argued, in one of his works in quantum physics, that complementarity was not only a philosophical superstructure but also the bedrock of quantum physics. Bohr's argument on the principle of complementarity stirred up epistemological debates in quantum physics. In fact, the Swiss-French journal "Dialectica" dedicated its autumn 1948 issue to the concept of complementarity—see pages 258-280 in Kalckar, Jorgen (Ed.). 1996. *Niels Bohr collected works: Foundations of quantum physics II (1933-1958) (Vol. 7).* Amsterdam, Netherlands: Elsevier Science B.V.

The Ikin and Ọpẹlẹ (technical) – These are the two most important divinatory instruments. While they are both pseudo-random number generators, capable of generating 256 binary signatures, the

Ikin is a sequential instrument, but the Ọpẹlẹ is a "one-shot" exponential instrument.

I classify the Ikin as a sequential instrument because it goes through eight sequential steps to generate a binary signature. However, the Ọpẹlẹ only goes through one step, making the Ọpẹlẹ a faster divinatory instrument than the Ikin. Logically, the Ikin operates based on the Boolean rule of odd and even binary counts—that is, f(x) = {a double mark (**II**), representing binary 1 if x = 1 (odd) else a single mark (**I**), representing binary 0 if x = 2 (even), or a blank if x < 1 or x > 2; where 0 ≤ x ≤ 16 and x is the number of nuts that remain in the left hand after an attempt is made to scoop all the 16 nuts, at once, with the right hand}. However, the Ọpẹlẹ operates based on the simple exponential power of 2—that is, $f(x) = 2^x$; where 0≤ x ≤ 8 and x represents the number of qutokens on the Ọpẹlẹ quantum chain. Note that the Ọpẹlẹ quantum chain can be modified in such a way that x is infinitely larger than 8.

The Old Ọyọ Kingdom – The most politically powerful and important Yoruba kingdom in history. While there is no consensus on when the Old Ọyọ Kingdom was founded, the general consensus, however, is that it fell in the 19th century CE. At its height, its tributaries spanned part of the South-West of Nigeria, the Republic of Benin and Togo.

Nupe Land – The closest Northern state to the Old Ọyọ Kingdom.

Yorubaland – The South-West region of modern-day Nigeria.

The Yoruba – The native inhabitants of Yoruba-land.

Eji – A Yoruba word meaning "two" in English.

Bibliography

Abimbola, Wande. 1997. *Ifa: An exposition of Ifa literary corpus.* New York, NY: Athelia Henrietta Press.

Abimbola, Wande. 1997. *Ifa will mend our broken world.* Roxbury, MA: Aim Books.

Adegbidin, Omotade. 2014. *Ifa in Yoruba thought system*. Durham, NC: Carolina Academic Press.

Adegbola, Tunde. 2011. "Transmission of scientific knowledge in Yoruba oral literature." In *Yoruba fiction, orature, and culture*, edited by Toyin Falola and Adebayo Oyebade, 27-40. Trenton, New Jersey: Africa World Press.

Adeeko, Adeleke. 2010. "Writing" and "Reference" in Ifa Divination Chants. *Oral Tradition,* 25(2): 283-303.

Ajala, Aderemi S. 2013. "Ifa divination: A diagnostic and therapeutic device in the Yoruba healing system." In *Reviewing reality: Dynamics of African divination,* edited by van Beek, Walter E.A. and Philip M. Peek, 115-138. Berlin, Germany: LIT VERLAG Dr. W. Hopf.

Ajayi, Bade. (n.d.). *A new model of Ifa binary system.* Retrieved from http://studylib.net/doc/7443994/a-new-model-of-ifa-binary-system

Ajayi, Bade. (n.d.). *Ifa Divinations: Its structure and application.* Retrieved from http://studylib.net/doc/16109287/divination-is-a-phenomenon-found-in-all-races-at-all...-i

Ajayi, Bade. (n.d.). *Ifa divination process.* Retrieved from http://studylib.net/doc/16109290/essays-in-honour-of-professor-wande-abimbola-1.-introduction

Alamu, F.O., Aworide, H.O., and Isharufe, W.I. 2013. "A comparative study on Ifa divination and computer science." *International Journal of Innovative Technology and Research,* 1(6): 524-528.

Agarwal, Kunal, Agarwal Karan, and Agrawal Shalini. 2017. "Quantum, Atomic and Nuclear Physics. A short review: Quantum computing." *Journal of Basic and Applied Engineering Research,* 4(6): 425-427.

Anderson, David L. (n.d.). *Computer types: Classical vs. non-classical*. Retrieved from http://www.mind.ilstu.edu/curriculum/nature_of_computers/computer_types.php

ASCII. 2002. In Microsoft computer dictionary (p. 36). 5th ed. Redmond, Washington: Microsoft Press.

Bascom, William. 1969. *Ifa divination: Communication between gods and men in West Africa.* Bloomington & Indianapolis, IN: Indiana University Press.

Bejide, Femi. 2015. "Mythology as veritable source of philosophy: A philosophical analysis of computer and Ifa divination techniques." *International Journal of Humanities and Social Studies,* 3(7): 187-193.

Binary Outcome. 2016. Retrieved from https://www.foxbusiness.com/markets/binary-outcome

Binsbergen, W. 1996. *The astrological origin of Islamic geomancy.* Retrieved from http://quest-journal.net/shikanda/ancient_models/BINGHAMTON%201996.pdf

Bit. 2002. In Microsoft computer dictionary (p. 61). 5th ed. Redmond, Washington: Microsoft Press.

Binary. 2002. In Microsoft computer dictionary (p. 57). 5th ed. Redmond, Washington: Microsoft Press.

Boolean and Boolean algebra. 2002. In Microsoft computer dictionary (p. 67). 5th ed. Redmond, Washington: Microsoft Press.

Byte. 2002. In Microsoft computer dictionary (p. 79). 5th ed. Redmond, Washington: Microsoft Press.

Campbell, Bolaji. 2016. “Of color, character, attributes, and values of Ọrunmila.” *Ifa divination, knowledge, power, and performance*, edited by Olupona, Jacob K. and Rowland O. Abiodun, 302-304. Bloomington, IN: Indiana University Press.

Connor, Steve. 2010. *The core of truth behind Sir Isaac Newton's apple.* Retrieved from https://www.independent.co.uk/news/science/the-core-of-truth-behind-sir-isaac-newtons-apple-1870915.html

Choosing, Deciding & Doing. (n.d.). Retrieved from http://www.psy.vanderbilt.edu/courses/psy216/ChoosingDecidingDoing.htm

Cuoco, Alex. 2014. *African narratives of Orishas, spirits and other deities*. Denver, CO: Outskirts Press.

Cusumano, Michael A. 2018. The Business of Quantum Computing. Retrieved from https://cacm.acm.org/magazines/2018/10/231363-the-business-of-quantum-computing/fulltext

Davis, Erik. 2010. *Nomad Codes: Adventures in modern Esoterica*. Portland, OR: YETI Books.

Eglash, Ron. 1999. *African Fractals: Modern computing and indigenous design*. New Brunswick, NJ: Rutgers University Press.

Fashina, Nelson. 2009. Replacing theory in African studies: Ifa literary corpus, origins, universality and the integration of epistemology. AEGIS Conference. Leizpig, Germany. June 4-7.

Fatunmbi, Fa'lokun. *(n.d.). Dafa: The Ifa concept of divination and the process of interpreting Odu.*
(n.c & s): Author.

Fatunmbi, Fa'lokun. 2015. *AWO: The Ifa concept of divination*. (n.c & s): Author.

Fisher, Tim. 2018. What is Hexadecimal? Retrieved from https://www.lifewire.com/what-is-hexadecimal-2625897

Folorunso, Olusegun, Adio T. Akinwale, Rebecca O. Vincent and Babatunde Olabenjo. 2010. "A mobile-based knowledge management system for "Ifa": An African traditional oracle." *African Journal of Mathematics and Computer Science Research,* 3(7): 114-131.

Ford, Clyde W. 1999. *The hero with an African face: Mythic wisdom of traditional Africa*. New York, NY: Bantam Books.

Freiberger, Marianne. 2015. *How does quantum computing work?* Retrieved from https://plus.maths.org/content/how-does-quantum-commuting-work

Greene, Tristan. (n.d.). *Understanding quantum computers: The basics.* Retrieved from https://thenextweb.com/artificial-intelligence/2018/03/15/understanding-quantum-computers-the-basics/

Hidalgo, Cesar. 2015. *Why information grows: The evolution of order, from atoms to economies.* New York, NY: Basic Books.

Hexadecimal. 2002. In Microsoft computer dictionary (p. 251). 5th ed. Redmond, Washington: Microsoft Press.

Johnson, Samuel. 2012. *The history of the Yorubas: From the earliest times to the beginning of the British protectorate.* Forgotten Books.

Karade, Baba I. 1994. *The handbook of Yoruba religious concepts*. Boston, MA: Weiser Books.

Kalckar, Jorgen (Ed.). 1996. *Niels Bohr collected works: Foundations of quantum physics II (1933-1958) (Vol. 7).* Amsterdam, Netherlands: Elsevier Science B.V.

Kenrick, Erik. 2015. *A primer on Knowledge? Rationalism vs Empiricism.* Retrieved from https://www.credocourses.com/blog/2015/a-primer-on-knowledge-rationalism-vs-empiricism/

Lande, Daniel R. 2014. "Development of the binary number system and the foundations of computer science." *The mathematics enthusiast,* 11(3): 513-540.

Longe, Olu. 1998. "Ifa divination and computer science." An inaugural lecture (delivered at the University of Ibadan, Nigeria, 22 December, 1983). Ibadan, Nigeria: Girardet Press.

Lodder, Jerry M. (n.d). *Binary Arithmetic: From Leibniz to Von Neumann.* Retrieved from https://pdfs.semanticscholar.org/4e42/8d4918e7da3ad c468c5b7cc3958b1fe21fc2.pdf

Mathew, George V. (n.d.). *Environmental psychology.* Retrieved from http://www.psychology4all.com/environmentalpsychology.htm

Marwala, Tshilidzi. (n.d.). *Semi-bounded rationality: A model for decision making.* Retrieved from https://www.researchgate.net/publication/236935969_Semi-bounded_Rationality_A_model_for_decision_making

Noaman M.N., and Quosy D. El. 2017. The hydrology of the Nile and ancient agriculture. *In Irrigated Agriculture in Egypt: Past, present and future,* edited by Satoh, Masayoshi and Aboulroos Samir, 9-28. Cham, Switzerland: Springer International Publishing.

Oluwole, Sophie B. 2017. *Socrates and Ọrunmila: Two patron saints of classical philosophy*. Lagos, Nigeria: Ark Publishers.

Odeyemi, Idowu. *What is Ifa?* (n.d.). Retrieved from https://www.scribd.com/document/398294567/What-is-Ifa-Idowu-Odeyemi

Pas, Heinrich. 2019. *Quantum monism could save the soul of physics*. Retrieved from https://blogs.scientificamerican.com/observations/quantum-monism-could-save-the-soul-of-physics/

Penrose, Roger. 1994. *Shadows of the mind: A search for the missing science of consciousness*. New York, NY: Oxford University Press.

Penrose, Roger. 1989. *The emperor's new mind.* New York, NY: Oxford University Press.

Pritchard, Duncan. 2018. *What is this thing called knowledge?* 4th ed. New York, NY: Routledge.

Qubit. 2002. In Microsoft computer dictionary (p. 433). 5th ed. Redmond, Washington: Microsoft Press.

Rafiquzzaman, Mohamed. 2014. *Fundamentals of digital logic and microcontrollers*. 6th ed. Hoboken, NJ: John Wiley & Sons, Inc.

Robert, Pelton. 1980. *The trickster in West Africa: a study of mythic irony and sacred delight*. Berkeley and Los Angeles, CA: University of California Press.

Salami, Ayo. 2002. *Ifa: A complete divination*. Lagos, Nigeria: NIDD Publishing and Printing Limited.

Sarma K J. 2015. "Understanding quantum computing." *International Journal of Scientific Engineering and Applied Science (IJSEAS),* 1(6): 370-388.

Savas, Niko. 2016. *Why do we use hexadecimal?* Retrieved from https://medium.com/@savas/why-do-we-use-hexadecimal-d6d80b56f026

Schneier, Bruce. 1996. *Applied cryptography: Protocols, Algorithms and source code in C.* 2nd ed. New York, NY: John Wiley & Sons, Inc.

Skinner, Stephen. (n.d.). *Terrestrial astrology: divination by geomancy*. London, Boston & Henley: Routledge & Kegan Paul.

Sugi, YK. 2018. *What is a quantum computer? Explained with a simple example.* Retrived from https://medium.freecodecamp.org/what-is-a-quantum-computer-explained-with-a-simple-example-b8f602035365

Segla, Aime. 2016. "Viewing formal mathematics from Yoruba conception of the sky." *Journal of Astronomy in Culture*, 1(1): 9-21.

Tate, Karl. 2013. How Quantum Entanglement Works (Infographic). Retrieved from https://www.livescience.com/28550-how-quantum-entanglement-works-infographic.html

Taiwo, Olufemi. 2016. "Kin n'ifa wi? Philosophical issues in Ifa Divination." In *Ifa divination, knowledge, power, and performance*, edited by Olupona, Jacob K., and Rowland O. Abiodun, 100-116. Bloomington, IN: Indiana University Press.

Taiwo, Afisi O. (n.d.). *Propensity probability and its application of knowledge in Ifa*. Retrieved from https://www.aau.at/wp-content/uploads/2018/04/KPF_Oseni-Taiwo-Afisi.pdf

Viznut. *The mystery of the binary* (n.d.). Retrieved from http://www.pelulamu.net/binmyst/

Whitener, Svetlana. 2017. *The difference between making a choice and a decision.* Retrieved from https://www.forbes.com/sites/forbescoachescouncil/2017/05/19/the-difference-between-making-a-choice-and-a-decision/#5f66b9bc4b7a

Woodford, Chris. 2018. How do computers work? A simple introduction. Retrieved from https://www.explainthatstuff.com/howcomputerswork.html

Index

Printed in Great Britain
by Amazon